lonely planet

HOW TO SURVIVE ANYTHING

HOW TO SURVIVE ANYTHING

A VISUAL GUIDE TO LAUGHING IN THE FACE OF ADVERSITY

ILLUSTRATED BY ROB DOBI

CONTENTS

FOREWORD

My name is Ed Stafford and I'm alive. Therefore, like you, I'm a survivor. I don't mean to be facetious — but there are many times in my life when I could have died.

In 2010 I became the first human to walk the length of the Amazon from source to sea. Four thousand miles, 860 days, seven pairs of boots, and one Guinness World Record. Before I set out (and all along the route) everyone told me I was going to die. On the way I was held up at arrow point by Asheninka Indians, at gun point by drugs traffickers, electrocuted by an electric eel, and arrested for suspected murder by Shipebo people. I suppose the naysayers were right — I could have died. But I didn't.

Fast forward two years and I chose to strand myself naked (and with nothing to help me survive) on an uninhabited island in the Pacific for 60 days. With no-one to talk to, I built an existence from scratch. Eating raw snails and coconuts eventually progressed to managing to light a fire and opening up new possibilities such as roasting feral goats' legs. I built myself a home in the trees and, after two months on my own, even plumbed it with guttering and a rainwater collection tank made from washed-up debris. I proved to myself that I could survive with nothing but two hands and half a brain.

Why do I take on such trips? Of course, I thrive off the adrenaline. But it's more than that. I was adopted as a baby, and that lies at the heart of it: I am genuinely grateful to have even been born. It could easily have been very different. I was lucky and I was given my crack at living a full life. We all are, I suppose. I have no intention of wasting it.

But things don't always go to plan. On one occasion in the Amazon, when I was over two weeks' walk from any human settlement, my GPS died. I wasn't sure if it was the unit or whether there had been a nuclear war as all the satellites had gone down. It didn't really matter. I had to make do with a 1:4,000,000 tourist map of South America and a cheap compass. There was such a high margin for error in my calculations each day that they were a joke. If it hadn't been life-threatening, it would have been hilarious. The advice in this book on how to survive in the wild without GPS (pages 130–133) might just have come in handy. Hindsight is a beautiful thing, as they say.

Sometimes, prevention is better than cure. I was once stranded naked in Rwanda without any form of sun protection, so I covered my head and shoulders in hippo faeces. It stopped me from burning and my girlfriend even commented on how smooth my skin was when I got home. Bonus.

My favourite survival trick is one I stole off an old expedition colleague of mine called Luke. Our plan, in the event that we encountered hostile tribes in the Amazon, was for Luke to whip out his juggling balls and start performing. We figured nobody would kill someone who was juggling. As a non-juggler I just hoped

that our assumption also stretched to jugglers' mates. Happily, we never had to find out.

But you don't have to be in a remote or hostile place to get into trouble. After a late night a few years ago (and feeling somewhat the worse for wear) I found myself locked out of my room in a Central London hotel with no clothes on (it does seems to be a recurring theme). With no desire to bare all in reception downstairs, I just called the lift and pressed the alarm button. As if by magic, a flustered employee fumbling a large set of room keys appeared. Phew. To those unfortunate enough to share this fate, there are some face-saving tips on pages 102–103.

For me survival has never been about He-Man strength or Boy Scout preparation. Nor do I think you need the courage of a bear or the cunning of a fox. I personally think you can survive any situation if you treat it like a game. Games require you to be focused and alert, but importantly they are just that: games. In this state of mind, you are less likely to freeze, or panic and make rash decision, or flap and do nothing. Your adrenaline will be channelled into constructive behaviour and the things you do will seem easier and more achievable. It seems a subtle change in outlook – but it's a very, very useful one.

Enjoy the book and, as the *SAS Survival Handbook* used to unhelpfully say, 'Can you survive? You have to!'

Thanks for that, chaps…

Ed Stafford
edstafford.org

HOW TO SURVIVE...

HOW TO SURVIVE AN
1 EARTHQUAKE

There are roughly 50 earthquakes around the world every day. Luckily, most of them are no great shakes, being minor or too small to feel. But there is always an exception, and the Big One could hit at any time.

1 Plan ahead. Channel your inner Boy Scout and stock up on non-perishable food, water, a battery-operated radio and fire extinguishers. Pack a bag with a first-aid kit, a pair of work gloves, a torch, some cash and a whistle.

2 Keep away from things that can fall on you. If an 8.5 quake hits while you're meditating in the middle of a field, you're in far less peril than you would be if a 6.5 were to strike while you were shopping in the bazaar in Mumbai.

3 Don't try to move or run outside. Drop to a more stable position, like your hands and knees, get underneath the most stable piece of furniture near you and hold on so it doesn't shake away from you. If you're in a car, stop and stay put (a car provides decent cover from falling debris).

4 Stay away from doorways. Once deemed strongpoints, they're now just considered places where you're more likely to have a swinging door slamming into your head.

5 Once the shaking stops, get to higher ground as soon as it's safe to do so as an even bigger quake could be on its way. If you're on the coast and an earthquake lasts more than 20 seconds, there's also a chance there will be a tsunami.

HOW TO SURVIVE A
SPACEWALK

The average astronaut gets to do only a handful of spacewalks in their lifetime. So if you get called upon to save the world *Armageddon*-style, be ready.

1 Pick up a good space skill. Astronauts are typically anything from ex-military to engineers to scientists. If you have an ability that can benefit the space station or the experiments they run there, you'll be a candidate.

2 Train for zero-g. Neutral-buoyancy training happens in a giant swimming pool containing a life-size replica of the space station. You suit up in an underwater version of a space suit and perform simulated tasks and repairs while floating, albeit experiencing far more drag than you would in space, which is a total vacuum.

3 Take a ride in the 'vomit comet'. NASA also uses a stripped-out 747 airplane to simulate zero-g, whereby pilots climb to a cruising altitude and then nosedive. The plane plummets for up to 30 seconds at a time, allowing astronauts to float around the fuselage, practising movements.

4 Learn your way around a space suit. A modern one weighs nearly 160kg (350lb) and contains up to 10 layers (including a diaper). The suits are basically mini spaceships, designed for up to eight hours' use, regulating temperature and condensation, pumping in oxygen and removing CO_2.

5 Get a taste of real space. Every astronaut is given about 15 minutes to get a feel for zero-g conditions before they undertake their first 'working' spacewalk. During this, you'll learn to 'translate', which means moving along the outside of the craft, hand over hand, very slowly and deliberately. Fast, clumsy movements can result in you losing a tool or, worse, floating into something that could damage your suit.

6 Wear sunscreen. Without an atmosphere to protect you, temperatures are about 150°C (300°F) in the sun, and -155°C (-250°F) in the shade. Your space suit will compensate for the extremes but conditions can still be intense.

7 Watch out for micro-meteorites. Like bullets whizzing through space, tiny pieces of meteors are common and have been known to rip through the hull of a space station – imagine what they'll do to a space suit.

8 Do *not* get separated from the space station. Technically, you're always wearing a retractable tether, but if that comes loose and you're even a millimetre beyond arm's length of the mother ship, you will simply keep floating away. Forever.

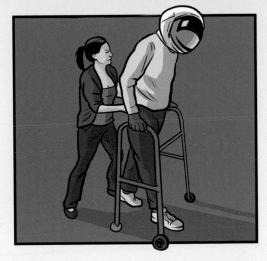

9 Master the jetpack. Astronauts wear a small nitrogen-powered jetpack for emergencies. But this has very limited fuel and battery and the controls are tricky to use. So, as if you were playing the most consequential video game of your life, aim for the ship and don't screw up.

10 Take time to recover. Spacewalking is mentally draining and the lack of gravity wreaks havoc on your body. After about a month in space you'll need physical rehab when you return to Earth, to rebuild muscle and regain balance.

HOW TO SURVIVE A
NIGHT IN THE SNOW

Winter can be as unforgiving as it is beautiful. If you enjoy venturing out into the snowy wilderness or going off piste, know what it takes to survive a night in the cold.

1 Do everything you can to get home, or at least to shelter. Call for help, walk to the nearest road and flag down a ride, or invite yourself into the nearest house.

2 Just in case you get stranded, every skier, winter walker and even car driver should consider carrying a basic snow-survival kit containing: chemical heat packs; a 30cm x 30cm (1ft x 1ft) piece of foam pad for insulation, two heavy-duty bin liners and a lighter.

3 Before you set out, check your gloves fit. If they are too tight they can restrict blood flow. To check, raise your arms and swing them as hard as you can towards the floor. If the mitts don't fly off, they're too snug.

4 Cut up your car seat. Foam torn from the seats and stuffed into your clothing will create insulation. Stay in the car — it offers great protection from the elements.

5 Put on the bin liners. You can reduce the effects of the wind and minimise moisture transfer by wearing one bag next to your skin and the other outside all your other layers.

6 Stay hydrated. If you're low on water, begin melting snow immediately. Do this by constantly adding about one-third snow to two-thirds existing water, and keeping it close to your body. Once it melts, drink off about a third of the water and repeat.

7 Build a fire. It may be tough to start a fire in winter conditions but in a survival situation you should try to burn anything you have that's flammable to keep warm, including fence posts or natural dead wood that's been kept covered and dry by a blanket of snow.

8 Make a bed and lie on it. Use any branches you can find – the more foliage the better – to create a mattress that is 25cm (10in) thick. Then insert several thinner 25cm- (10in-) long sprigs into your mattress vertically so it will maintain maximum height when you sit or lie on it.

9 Leave snow caves to the experts (and polar bears). You have to expend a lot of energy to make one, so you're better off saving your breath. If you do build one, make it small.

10 Cuddle up, if you can. If you're stranded with a partner, hunker down for the night back-to-back. It not only offers the best heat transfer, you can also sense if the other person falls asleep.

11 Stay awake. Your metabolic rate drops considerably when you're sleeping. Do isometric exercises such as pressing your back into your partner's. Star jumps (jumping jacks) help get the blood flowing to your hands and feet.

HOW TO SURVIVE
SUPERGLUE ACCIDENTS

Invented by accident during World War II when manufacturers were trying to create clear gun sights, superglue was later brought to market as an ultra-strong adhesive. It's been gluing people's fingers to broken coffee mugs ever since.

1 Use superglue for serious fixes only. Cyanoacrylate – the chemical name for the adhesive – is no joke. It can bear a load of up to a tonne, if bonding metal to metal. It can be used to fix just about anything but the bond is always strongest between less porous materials.

2 Be careful around clothing. Not only will it ruin it, but chemicals in superglue have been known to react with natural fibres such as cotton, wool and leather, releasing a heat so intense it can smoke and cause burns.

3 Keep it away from your skin – unless you have a cut or are a rock climber. It may not be medically recommended, but superglue is so good at closing up a wound that Army medics use it on the battlefield. Climbers and guitar players put the glue on their fingertips to decrease sensitivity.

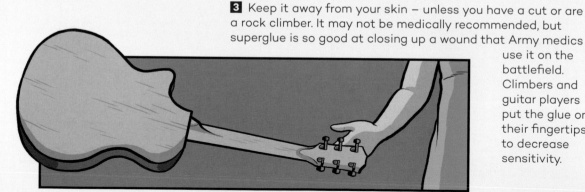

4 If you do get in a sticky situation, roll with it. First, try to separate your skin from the item it's adhered to by rolling it off slowly. This will minimise the surface area and make the separation less painful.

5 Keep some nail-polish remover to hand. Acetone is the most effective compound for softening and removing superglue. Coincidentally, a nail emery board is a pretty effective tool for rubbing away stubborn glue.

6 Go natural. If you like to live chemical-free (though you probably wouldn't be using superglue in the first place), everything from margarine to salt to dishwashing powder is also said to soften cyanoacrylate.

A rip current can occur anywhere there are waves, including giant lakes. The bigger the waves, the more powerful the rip.

1 Know what to look for. The water inside a rip current is often foamier or more churned up than the water around it, sometimes even brownish in colour, having stirred up sand or dirt. If there are lifeguards around, ask them where the rips are – they probably spotted every one of them before they were even done with their morning coffee.

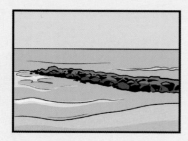

2 Pay attention to piers and jetties. Man-made structures like these often form the trough in the sand that creates a rip current. Troughs can form naturally, too, and they can also appear, disappear, or change throughout the day.

3 Unless your name is Michael Phelps, steer clear. A rip current can travel at around 8kph (5mph) – about twice as fast as you can swim. If you're a surfer, you can use a rip to get beyond the breakers faster, riding it like a conveyor belt out to sea. But, unless you're lifeguard-fit, you have little chance of out-swimming a rip.

4 If you do get caught, go with the flow. Relax, tread water, and let the rip pull you away from shore — you'll need to save your strength. As soon as you feel the current ease, swim parallel to the shore. Rips are narrow channels and you will often exit the current if you move laterally.

5 Still stuck? Sit tight. The rip current will only pull you out so far and will sometimes even deliver you to the calmer water behind the breaking waves. Once there, do what you can to get the attention of a lifeguard.

HOW TO SURVIVE A
6 SPAGHETTI SUPPER (WITHOUT THE SPLATTERS)

Mamma mia! Italians are so opinionated about the *right* way to eat spaghetti, it should probably be an article of their constitution.

1 First, cook it correctly. Good spaghetti etiquette starts with cooking the pasta just right. Too *al dente* and the strands won't wrap around and stick to the others as you twirl. Beware, overcooked spaghetti is deemed equally offensive, as is breaking the noodles before boiling them.

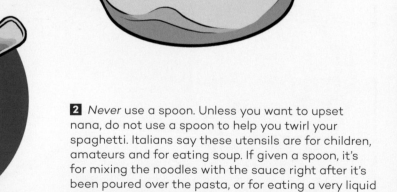

2 *Never* use a spoon. Unless you want to upset nana, do not use a spoon to help you twirl your spaghetti. Italians say these utensils are for children, amateurs and for eating soup. If given a spoon, it's for mixing the noodles with the sauce right after it's been poured over the pasta, or for eating a very liquid sauce (as is often served with angel hair pasta).

3 Master the twirl. Separate some strands from the pile, stab your fork into them, then twirl your fork so all the pasta strands wraps around it. Proper distribution of sauce will ensure the strands stick to each other so everything stays in place.

4 Never cut or bite the pasta. The trick is to start your twirl with an amount of pasta that will create the perfect-size mouthful, i.e. one that will go into your mouth cleanly and doesn't require any slurps, sucking or biting to cut away excess pasta.

5 Don't mention bread, cheese or bowls. Whether bread should be served with pasta or not, which type of cheese should accompany it, and if it should be served in a shallow bowl or on a plate are debates that have been raging across Italy for centuries. Unless you think you can hold your own, leave it alone.

HOW TO SURVIVE
OFFENDING A MAFIA DON

7

Pssst, there's a guy who knows a guy who says he can tell you all you need to know about holding your own in the presence of a mob boss. Here's the lowdown...

1 Pick a good nickname. Adding a 'y' to the end – Sammy, Jimmy, Tommy – is a good start, but it's even better if you can incorporate a reference to a physical trait: One-eye Louis, Fingers Freddy, No-neck Sal, etc.

2 Learn the lingo. The boss is called a capo, his boss is a don; if you have a problem and want to talk with the boss, say you have a 'beef' and would like a 'sit-down'.

3 Get made. If you've impressed your new amigos, you may get invited into the 'family', a ritual known as 'getting made'. Expect a very tense sit-down with the capos and the don, during which a picture of a saint is burned and blood is drawn from your trigger finger.

4 Take the code of silence. Also known as an 'omerta', this 'blood oath' of silence and allegiance is more important than your wedding vows. The penalty for stepping out of line? You'll be knocked off, of course.

5 If you're called upon for a favour, drop everything, immediately. Being part of *the family* is believed to be more important than religion and even your real family. And never disrespect women, especially your wife. This rule goes way back to the beginnings of the Sicilian mafia and remains a central tenet today in Italy and the USA.

6 Be entrepreneurial, but not *too* entrepreneurial. Never start your own racket without the permission of local capos.

8

HOW TO SURVIVE A
BLIND DATE

Fraught with peril, blind dates can be nerve-wracking, exhilarating, cringeworthy, magical, or all of the above. Happily there are a few things you can do to prevent it from being a *total* disaster.

1 The first rule of blind-dating club is to not judge a person before you get the chance to *actually* judge them. Let's be honest, the days of the fully blind date are over. You've Google-stalked each other at least once pre that awkward first meeting, so act surprised, yeah?

2 Just because you've never met, doesn't mean you can't talk to each other first. This isn't *Pride and Prejudice*. There don't need to be church elders present. Drop them a text, establish some common ground. NB: This gives you the chance to slip in a mention of that thing you might have to go to after the date: ie – your built-in get-out clause.

3 Come to the table with a couple of killer questions and conversation-prompting answers. Less 'where do you see yourself in five years', more 'what's the most embarrassing thing you've ever done at a Christmas party?' Never talk about yourself for more than four or five minutes. NB: do not use a phone to time this though.

4 Mirror their body language. It's a way of saying 'I am like you, I feel the same'. Speak at the same pace, use the same tone – make eye contact. Note, if used incorrectly, this can be really, *really* creepy.

5 Keep your phone away. A study from the University of Essex shows just the act of putting a mobile on the table between you and a partner negatively impacts on the quality of the conversation.

6 Even if they're not your type, play nice. They might have friends who are...

HOW TO SURVIVE A
9 TSUNAMI

Every coastline on earth has the potential to be hit by a tsunami, but some places are far more vulnerable than others. The 'Ring of Fire' is made up of all the countries surrounding the Pacific Ocean, all of which have large tectonic plates off their coastlines. This the most active tsunami zone in the world – big-wave central.

1 Have faith in technology. Many tsunami-prone countries now have an early-warning system. If there's danger, you'll hear sirens, emergency instructions on the radio and TV, and possibly even receive a text.

2 If the alarm sounds, drop everything and get to higher ground. A tsunami travels about as fast as a plane. If it's discovered further out, you could have as much as an hour to reach safety; if it's just a few miles off shore, you have less than five minutes to react.

3 If you're on a beach without a warning system, the only indication you may get of impending doom will be a dramatic receding of the ocean away from the shore. If the wave is simply too close to out-run, get yourself to the top of the sturdiest-looking building or tree near you and hold fast.

4 If you are torn away from whatever you were clinging on to, swim towards anything large that floats. Try to 'surf' (or at least stay) on top of the object rather than clutching the side, to avoid being crushed by debris.

5 Pretend you are a limpet, stick to your buoy like glue and watch out for the next surge. Tsunamis are often followed by a second – and sometimes larger – wave, so don't leave whatever safety you have found until you are 100 per cent sure you're out of danger.

HOW TO SURVIVE
10 PUBLIC SPEAKING

Unlearn the 'rules' of public speaking. Authenticity is more important than anything else and rules can make you act unnaturally. You want to seem like an expert in whatever you're talking about, not a pro at public speaking.

1 Treat a presentation like you would a date. It's about connecting with people, being yourself and not being a bore. The more likeable and approachable you are, the more effective you will be at conveying information.

2 Watch TED Talks. These online think-tank presentations show how passion for a subject overrides performance. Some of the smartest, most dynamic people in the world are not necessarily great public speakers.

3 Video yourself. But do *not* critique every detail – use film to spot the most obvious issues, like the overuse of filler words such as 'um' or 'like', or to catch distracting hand gestures. Or try it out on a small audience of friends. Get them to ask you difficult questions afterwards.

4 Dress the part. For formality and authority, don a suit; if you want your presentation to have a more free-form feel, dress more casually. Most importantly, wear something that helps your audience relate to you.

5 Embrace nervousness. You can still give a great presentation if you're nervous, and acknowledging it, to your audience or just to yourself, often minimises it. View it as being excitement directed inwards, to be channelled outwards into animation and passion.

6 Nail the first 10 minutes. Nervousness usually subsides after the first few minutes, so spend most of your prep time practising the beginning of your talk. Or kick it off in a way that helps you relax, such as by asking questions, doing a physical demonstration or telling a story.

HOW TO SURVIVE
11 THE MIDDLE SEAT SQUEEZE ON A LONG-HAUL FLIGHT

It's a packed plane and you've just drawn the short, squashed straw: a middle seat. How do you wriggle your way out of this one?

1 Always choose your airline carefully. Check out the seat dimensions online first (try www.seatguru.com), and never settle for a width of less than 43cm (17in) and a pitch of under 76cm (30in).

2 Board as early as you can. Not only are you psychologically establishing your territory, you're ensuring you get space in the overhead locker. Put the bare essentials under the seat in front of you: an extra layer, a book, your headphones and water.

3 Pack Bluetooth headphones. Not only will these *not* get tangled with those of your neighbour, they'll allow you to walk around the cabin unhindered, still listening to your music. As an added bonus, they tend to be better at noise cancelling if you're trying to sleep (or shut out the chatty fatty on your right-hand side).

4 Identify and befriend the senior cabin-crew member. Their powers include the allocation of spare seats. There are always no-shows before take-off, and that spells an opportunity for wily travellers. As soon as everyone's on board, locate this individual and enquire politely about extra seats. If you don't ask you don't get.

5 Take tactical toilet breaks. You don't want to be clambering over sleeping bodies with a bursting bladder. If your neighbour goes, you go. Otherwise, time your (*ahem*) movement so it occurs shortly before or after the meal service, when the majority of passengers will be awake – and you won't get caught behind the trolley.

6 Invest in a neck pillow. They're comfy, they aid sleep and, most importantly, they help you establish your personal space. Now drift off, you'll be there in no time...

HOW TO SURVIVE
SUNBURN

12

We've all been there – you spend a touch too long in the sun and before you know it you resemble a lobster, and not in a delectable-treat way. The saying 'prevention is better than a cure' couldn't be more true in sunbathing situations, so before you fry yourself to a crisp, follow a few simple rules and avoid the big burn.

1 Use broad-spectrum sunscreens that provide protection from both UVA and UVB rays. Don't be fooled by high SPF numbers. SPF 15 blocks 93 per cent of harmful rays; SPF 30 blocks 97 per cent. Anything higher than 50 offers a negligible benefit.

2 Avoid sitting in the sun for prolonged periods of time, especially between 11am and 3pm. The amount of sun your skin can safely stand will depend on your colouring, so be sensible and don't overdo it.

3 Despite claims, no sunscreen is waterproof. The best ones are water-*resistant* for up to 80 minutes, so if you're swimming or sweating you should apply cream more frequently.

4 Stay away from sprays as 50 per cent flies away in the wind. If you do use one, rub the sunscreen around to ensure you are covered. Stay away from the BBQ – most spray sunscreens are alcohol-based and highly flammable.

5 Treat a burn before you feel it. If you're looking a little pink, it will turn red within a few hours. Sunburns draw moisture out of the body towards the skin, so start drinking water or sports drinks to keep yourself hydrated.

6 Soothe your skin. First take some ibuprofen to cut the pain and reduce inflammation. Next, take a cool bath or shower to relieve the sting, and (gently!) slap on aloe or a hydrating moisturiser, ideally containing vitamins E and C.

HOW TO SURVIVE
13 LOSING YOUR CHILD IN A CROWD

Your heart is racing, you feel faint and sick – it can only mean one thing: your child has vanished. Nearly all children who get lost in a crowd are found fairly quickly, but here are some preparatory measures you can take should your offspring go AWOL.

1 Choose bright clothing. Dress your child in colours that make them stand out in a crowd. This also helps strangers spot them if people are searching.

2 Make them say cheese! Once your child is dressed, snap a picture – a recent photo is the first thing officials will ask for if you report your child missing.

3 Make a simple plan that kids will remember when they are panicked. The number-one rule is to stay put. The 'mummy' principle is also useful, as mothers are easy for your child to spot and are likely to be a safe resource that will notify someone official.

4 Slip a piece of paper in your child's pocket listing your number and any important allergies before you go out. Do NOT include or advertise your child's name, as this will make it easier for strangers to lure them away.

5 Keep cool. The moment you realise you may have misplaced your child, retrace your steps to where you last saw them, call their name and ask passers-by if they've seen them. Don't go wandering off – they will be trying to find you too.

6 Sound the alarm. If your child is not found in just a few minutes, alert a security guard and a manager. If that doesn't work, notify the police. Most countries have special police alerts for these situations.

HOW TO SURVIVE
LOSING YOUR HAIR

Shedding hair at an alarming rate? You are not alone. Around 65 per cent of men and 40 per cent of women in their mid-thirties experience significant hair loss and see their once-lustrous locks clogging up their combs.

1 First, blame mum *and* dad. Hair loss is largely a result of genetics, caused by baldness genes that are passed down on both sides, so you can spread the blame.

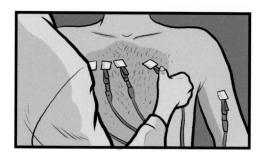

2 Make sure the moulting is not an indication of an underlying issue, such as stress or disease. While neither necessarily *causes* shedding, they speed up the process considerably. Treat these, and the hair loss will at least stop, and some hair may even grow back.

3 Take care of what you've got. What's gone is gone, but experts say you can slow further loss if your hair is weak by avoiding high-heat treatments like colouring, ironing and excessive blow-drying, eating well (lots of Omega-3 fatty acids, found in fish and nuts) and using nourishing hair products.

4 Wear a hat. It won't prevent the balding process, but it won't accelerate it either. And you'll look stylish in the meantime.

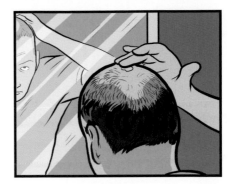

5 Ignore the hair-loss hucksters. All but two products out there that claim to 'regrow' hair are mere snake oils. Finasteride (for men) or Minoxidil (for women) do work (sort of). Marketed under names like Proscar or Propecia and Rogaine, these have been proven to not only stop hair loss but also to bring *some* hair back. Be warned, like most marriages, they don't come cheap, you have to commit to them for life and they come with a laundry list of side effects.

6 Borrow some hair from your back. The latest treatment for hair loss is transplant surgery, whereby doctors take follicles from another part of your body and transplant them on to your head. Most agree that this is the most natural-looking and permanent solution. More hair on your head, less on your back? It's win-win, really.

HOW TO SURVIVE A
15 BORDER CROSSING

Border crossings can be intimidating hives of corruption, bureaucracy, and lawlessness. In some countries all you need for a smooth ride is a clean criminal record – but not all.

1 Prepare in advance. Make sure you have the correct visas and spare passport photos, and fill out any forms ahead of time. Stop in the largest town before the border to get the lowdown on when border officials take their siesta and whether there are any short cuts.

2 Carry plenty of cash, some in the currency of the country you're entering, so you can move through town quickly.

3 Look the part. If you're headed to a music festival or full-moon party, don't dress like you are. The goal is to fit in. Dress too smart and you'll be singled out as someone who can afford bribes; too shabby and you'll look like someone agents are paid to keep out of the country.

4 Submit to the power trip and smile. Border officials have a reputation for letting you know who's boss. Let them feel like they are in charge, don't question extra 'fees' that are tacked on last minute (unless they are unreasonably high), and don't get rattled.

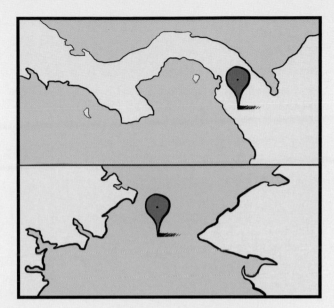

5 Avoid the two worst border crossings in the world. The Darién Gap, between Colombia and Panama, is crawling with armed narco-traffickers and guerrillas: neither country wants you entering here. If you travel from Alaska to Russia via the Bering Sea there's a very good chance you will be detained and questioned.

6 Once through a checkpoint, head straight for a waiting bus, pre-arranged ride or pre-booked hotel. Borders are the worst places in which to look lost, confused or as if you want to hear about your options from a 'friendly' local.

HOW TO SURVIVE
STRESS

We need stress. Without it, why would we bother doing anything? However, when being a bit edgy and über-alert morphs into a case of jittery incompetence, it's time to seek help.

1 Being organised is the best stress-buster. Stress happens when you can't control what's happening, so get a diary and use it.

2 Write a list of people on whom you can call for help if you do lose it, and let them know if you are feeling the pressure.

3 Identify situations you find taxing and accept them for what they are. Christmas, work parties, speeches, shopping trips – they won't change for you, so if you want to avoid them, just do it. Never complain, never explain.

4 Just say no. When you know something is going to make you stressed, just refuse politely. This has triple benefits: the chance to dodge something irritating, a feeling of confidence and control, and more time to do the things you actually like.

5 When stress rears its ugly head, go outside and walk it off straight away. The fresh air, sun and exercise will all work together to calm your mood and give you the time to decide your next move.

6 Go somewhere quiet. Studies have shown than long-term exposure to loud noise elevates blood pressure and stress hormones, raising your risks of heart attack by 10 per cent. A small, well-insulated room, or even noise-cancelling headphones, will work wonders.

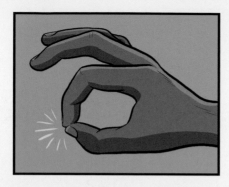

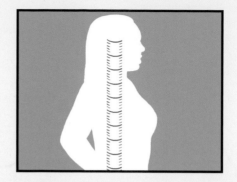

7 Recall an instance when you felt serene and relaxed. When the memory peaks, clasp your thumb and forefinger together, releasing them when the recollection dissipates. Next time you need calm, clasp your fingers again to fire off a neurological stimulus.

8 Visualise a blood-pressure gauge inside your body. Take note of the level it is at currently, then as you take some deep breaths in through your nose and out through your mouth, see this gauge dropping down and feel a calm sensation run throughout your body.

9 Write down tomorrow's tasks before you leave the office, ranked in order of importance, and label each with the time it will take to complete. You'll see that the mountain is actually a molehill and you can go home and forget about it.

10 Remember the Pareto Principle and apply it to situations that stress you out. Pareto discovered that 80 per cent of results come from 20 per cent of your efforts. It's why you get more done in the first two hours of your day, and why the best people tend to leave parties earlier.

11 Chin up. How we hold ourselves physically affects how we feel psychologically. If you smile and laugh with your head up and shoulders back, your state of mind will soon change.

12 Make time for intimacy at bedtime for a burst of natural sleep hormones, and talk to your partner about everything that's been on your mind. A problem shared is a problem halved.

17 BEING LOST IN THE DESERT

While low deserts like the Sahara are extremely harsh and contain few survival aids, the more common high desert – anywhere above 762m (2500ft), such as Joshua Tree National Park, much of Utah and the Atacama Desert – has everything you need to survive, if you know where to look.

1 Cover up. Before you do anything, build a shelter and/or cover exposed areas of skin. Makeshift sunscreen can be made from mud, ground-up roots or the white powder found on Aspen trees – use anything that creates a barrier between you and the rays.

2 Keep your cool. Evaporative cooling is one of the most efficient ways to regulate temperature. Lightly wet some fabric and wrap it around your neck so it has direct contact with your jugular blood flow.

3 Drink up. Your body uses up to 2L of water per day, so begin to preserve the water you have and start hunting for fresh supplies. Whatever you do, don't over-ration – instead, drink small sips throughout the day.

4 Take up dowsing. To find water, survey the landscape – water travels from high to low ground. Also, look for a spot where the tracks of several animals converge or where the vegetation changes from dry scrub to a deeper green.

5 Make your own watering hole. If you can't find water, don't panic – plants drink during the day, often depleting whatever water is present. At night, the water table rises again. Dig a large hole at a likely spot and water will begin to pool inside it.

6 Bed down. Finally, do what you can to stay warm at night. The key is to create a barrier between you and the ground. Air is a terrible conductor, so the more 'airy' the layer, the warmer you'll stay.

HOW TO SURVIVE
18 GRIEF

Grief can follow the loss of just about anything significant in one's life – a loved one, a relationship, even a career. While there is no right or wrong way to grieve, psychologists are in agreement that it's best to just let it happen. So grab a box of tissues, close the shutters and give yourself a break: big girls (and boys) *do* cry.

1 Welcome grief with open arms. It is one of the most normal human emotions there is. Treat it like a scab: no picking, let it do its job. The five stages of grief – denial, anger, bargaining, depression, acceptance – do *not* represent a ticklist to happiness. Many psychiatrists say that this oversimplifies things and that you could experience all of them, none of them, or just a few and in no particular order.

2 Do not get in grief's way. People turn to everything from drugs and alcohol to work and hobbies to stave off the feelings that come with grieving. Anything at all that inhibits the flow of raw emotions is simply putting the process on hold and prolonging the agony.

3 Make time to mourn. Many cultures have a designated mourning period following the loss of a loved one. This is when you should just allow yourself to fall apart, ignore the other important things in your life, and be a blubbering mess.

4 Re-imagine your memories. An American writer once said, 'death is the end of a life, not a relationship'. After losing someone, try to focus on the happy memories of your time with them. Also, separate the remembrance of loss from the things you enjoy that remind you of the one you mourn. These new memories will feel bittersweet – let that become your new norm.

5 However, if the emotions are *too* intense, seek out a little extra help. Up to 10 per cent of people experience something known as 'complex' grief, in which the depression doesn't evolve and lasts much longer than expected. There are people who can help in these instances, so don't be afraid to issue a Mayday.

6 Find closure. Many psychiatrists subscribe to a three-step therapy whereby you begin by talking about the day the person died. Next, imagine a conversation with that person and role play their responses (this works through unresolved issues). Finally, bring the grieving back to yourself, focusing on the future and what is still possible.

7 Beware of *that* day. The anniversary of someone's death will always trigger emotions, even if this is unconscious. Let it happen and stay in touch with those emotions. Consider this further healing.

HOW TO SURVIVE A
19 SNAKEBITE

Around 100,000 people around the world die from snakebites every year, and twice as many are permanently disabled. However, it's not always the bite that does victims in – it's incorrect treatment or a lack of antivenom, or even road or domestic accidents caused by the mere sight of a snake.

1 Suss out your serpents. Learn which are the deadly critters before you venture into snake territory, so you can avoid them where possible and tell medical staff which species bit you if they do attack. Read up on how to behave during encounters with specific types of snakes (whether to freeze or run away) and how best to treat the different bites.

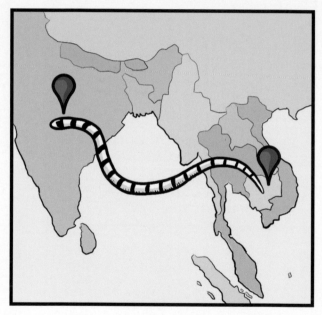

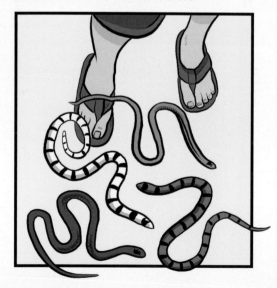

2 Do your research and find out which hospitals hold the best, most relevant, antivenoms. In poorer Southeast Asian countries, such as Cambodia, the population relies on antivenoms developed for snake species in India and these may be stored thousands of miles away.

3 If you are bitten, slowly move away from the snake if necessary, otherwise stay still and try to be calm. Keep the injury below your heart where possible. Panicking and rushing around will only speed the course of the venom through your body.

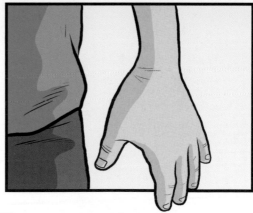

4 Call for help and get to a hospital. Don't try to use an elastic bandage for pressure immobilisation (unless you are certain which type of snake bit you and that it is safe and advisable to do so) or to incise the wound with a razor. Don't eat or drink anything at all.

5 Remove any jewellery or constricting clothing, in anticipation of swelling. Other symptoms can include pain, speech impairment, drooling and loss of balance and these may occur 10–30 minutes after the injury.

20

HOW TO SURVIVE
MEETING THE IN-LAWS

The moment you have been dreading has arrived. The early days of the relationship are over and it's time to meet the in-laws. The aim of the game is to make them like you, without being too over-eager to please. Or offensive.

1 Keep it simple. If you're hosting, don't attempt to pull off culinary pyrotechnics. You will end up singeing an eyebrow, baking a utensil into the food or punching your other half in the face because they opened the oven and ruined your soufflé.

2 If you're going to them, carve out a wedge of time when it'll be just you and your partner. Yes, the parents will wonder what you're up to, but breathing space is vital, for everyone. These meetings can get very claustrophobic.

3 Do your homework. Find out from your other half what their parents' weak points are and what they value above all else. Forewarned is forearmed. If there is something in your past that might come up, have a pre-packaged answer up your sleeve. NB: remember, they are being interviewed too. Do *not* be afraid to deflect awkward questions with, well, more questions.

4 *Always* bring a gift. As much as your other half might protest, take an inexpensive but thoughtful offering. Wine and flowers first, chocolates and 'something for the garden' at the next visit. Stay away from personalised or gendered gifts until you know them better. Then feel free to crack out the 'I'm with stupid' T-shirt...

5 Don't be *too* enthusiastic about presents they get you, or you could end up being given a candle, scarf or dish towel set for every birthday and Christmas forever more. A polite and modestly enthusiastic 'thank you very much' will suffice.

21

HOW TO SURVIVE
FOOD POISONING

There are few moments in life less dignified than an explosive bout of food poisoning. But if you know what's coming, you may have just enough time to get yourself to a safe place to let 'er rip.

1 Boil it, cook it, peel it or forget it. To minimise your chances of eating dodgy food, this old chestnut still holds true. The docs also say you should add 'carry hand sanitiser' to the list and wash your hands frequently. The most common culprits for food poisoning are uncooked meats, unpasteurised milk or human-contaminated food.

2 Ride it out. Most pathogens start to cause discomfort within a few hours and run their course in 12–48 hours. Standard symptoms include cramps, diarrhoea, fever, chills, headache, nausea, vomiting and weakness.

3 Preserve a little poop. If you want to know exactly what's causing your suffering – and you'd have to *really* want to know – take a stool sample to a doctor for analysis.

4 Do *not* get dehydrated. Along with the 2L (3½ pints) of water you should be drinking every day anyway, sip an additional 200ml (7fl oz) fluid each time you are sick. Wait 10–15 minutes and drink slowly, or you'll bring it all back up again. You can make your own rehydration solution by stirring 2.5ml (½ tsp) each of bicarb soda (baking soda) and salt along with 60mL (4 tbs) sugar into 1L (1.75 pints) water.

5 Know when to call in the cavalry. If you don't get better within 48 hours, your fever tops 38°C (101°F) or you notice any blood in your stool, see a doctor immediately.

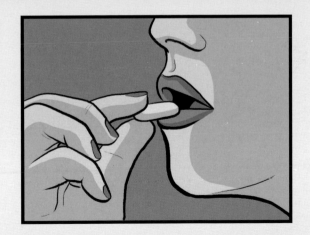

6 Kill it with pills. Prescribed antibiotics are the safest and quickest way to treat a bad strain of food poisoning.

HOW TO SURVIVE
22 THE SEVEN-YEAR ITCH

Originally a medical term used to describe the life cycle of irritating skin problems, the seven-year itch often spells relationship catastrophe. In the USA, the length of the average marriage is, you guessed it, about seven years.

1 Don't despair. Psychologists believe that seven-year itches coincide with our natural rhythm of development. It's quite normal to have seven- to nine-year spells of stability, followed by a couple years of uncertainty.

2 Keep your 'house' clean. A marriage is like moving into a new house: at first, it's new and exciting. But, along with your baggage, you bring in a little clutter and store it in the spare room. Over time, junk piles up until you're living in the hallway. That's when you think it's time for a new house.

3 Don't get distracted by bugbears. Leaving the toilet seat up may be a sore point, but it's not make-or-break important. Identify the real issues and don't be afraid to talk about them.

4 Reassess the contract. When starting a relationship, you find someone who meets a need you have at that moment in your life. But that was then: whatever contract you entered into may now be obsolete.

5 Spice things up. Not just in the bedroom, either. As spontaneity wears off make time to cultivate new experiences –travelling, throwing dinner parties, or just going out more often.

6 Draw up a new contract with your *new* vision for the future. If it matches up with your partner's, you're in luck. If not, this might not be an itch that can be scratched.

23 HOW TO SURVIVE A HANGOVER

Until scientists discover a cure for the common hangover – and I think we can all agree they should speed things up a little – you'll just have to outsmart the symptoms.

1 Prevention is the best cure, so before you even start drinking, eat. A lot. Eating may be cheating, but a full stomach slows the absorption of alcohol into your bloodstream. And drink water: most people don't drink enough water throughout the day and heavy boozing simply exacerbates dehydration.

2 Stick to clear spirits. Some scientists say that ethanol combined with the congeners found in dark booze, created by ageing and fermentation, are more toxic than ethanol alone, as found in vodka. Bourbon has nearly 40 times more congeners than vodka.

3 By the time you wake up, the alcohol will have metabolised into acetaldehyde, which causes the familiar symptoms: dizziness, nausea, headache and stomach problems. Attack the toxin with taurine. Soft drinks in general are good because they replace depleted glucose, but energy drinks that contain taurine have been shown to boost the liver enzyme that breaks down acetaldehyde.

4 Pop some pills. Take aspirin, but avoid paracetamol. Ibuprofen will reduce inflammation and relieve your headache, but paracetamol overworks your already beleaguered liver and can become more toxic than the alcohol itself.

5 Eat. Again. Alcohol seriously depletes blood sugar, so it's important to replace it as soon as possible by throwing down a big brunch.

6 When all else fails, have another drink. Most scientists say that hair-of-the-dog will simply mask the symptoms and prolong your misery. However, others point out that part of the pain is a minor case of withdrawal. A little top-up might be just what you need to get over the hangover hump.

HOW TO SURVIVE A
TODDLER'S TANTRUM

Red face. Beating fists. Shrieking cries. To you, a tantrum seems out of proportion and unjust, but to your little one it is the end of the world, and they need you to help them get through it.

1 Be strategic. You can avoid the tantrum altogether by knowing the triggers and swerving them if possible. If your toddler always has a meltdown in the supermarket, shop online.

2 Give them some choice but stay in control. Start by having clear routines, with meals, naps, bath and bed at a set time. Within that framework, give them some control over what to eat, wear and play with.

3 Read the warning signs. Hunger, thirst, tiredness, jealousy and frustration can all be triggers. When your toddler starts to show the first signs of a tantrum you may be able to head it off with a banana, some juice, a nap, a swift exit from the baby group or just a massive cuddle.

4 If things are starting to kick off, try distraction. Your toddler has a short attention span, so use it to your advantage. 'Ooh, look at that doggy/plane/ladybird!' will go a long way at this age.

5 Don't add fuel to the fire. Once your toddler is in full tantrum mode, so long as it is safe to do so, walk away and give them some space. Like a blaze, it will burn itself out more quickly if nothing else is added to the equation. 'I'll be in the living room when you're ready for a cuddle' might be a good parting comment.

6 In public places such as the supermarket, post office or a china shop, it is sometimes best to just pick up your child and go outside to minimise your embarrassment, and the damage that your little bull could do... Less stress for you means less stress for them too.

7 Time-out works for you as well as for them. Calmly putting your child in a boring environment away from stimuli – such as a bottom step, playpen or pushchair – for a few minutes can help by removing the factors that caused the tantrum.

8 Keep calm. 'Emotional containment' is the process by which you support a child to process their overwhelming feelings through role-modelling. When they lose it, you hold it together yourself. Scream silently into a towel in the other room before smiling sweetly and saying calmly 'You seem really cross about that.' Use calming techniques to lower your own stress levels – deep breathing, relaxing your muscles, repeating positive talk inside your head: 'I will keep calm'. You can do it.

9 Your co-parent is your wing-man. A subtle eye roll across a room at a knowing and sane other adult can be a lifesaver, even if they're not rushing to your rescue.

10 Don't forget to refuel once it is over. Cake, wine, beer, chocolate – all are recommended for purely medicinal purposes. For you, obviously.

HOW TO SURVIVE
25 **iDENTITY THEFT**

Out on the cyber-seas of our information age lurk privacy pirates who want to come onboard and hijack your personal details. Be warned, be prepared and defend yourself from attack.

1 Become a human Fort Knox. Never use public computers to access sensitive information; avoid carrying things like a national identity card, passport, or credit cards you don't use regularly; and, finally, install good antivirus software and anti-spyware on your computer.

2 Keep your most important documents under lock and key. A desk drawer simply isn't good enough for preventing them from slipping into the wrong hands.

3 Shred everything. These days, identity thieves are as likely to rummage through your mail and rubbish as they are your emails.

4 Face it, your pet's name is *not* a password. Yes, it's annoying having to remember a dozen different passwords, each full of symbols, capital letters, and numbers. But you are extremely vulnerable if you use one or two simple passwords for everything. There are secure apps out there that will organise passwords for you so you don't have to remember them.

5 Beware of medical-identity theft. Thieves commonly appropriate someone else's identity in order to get hold of prescription drugs or free medical assistance. This can be especially dangerous if, for instance, you end up needing blood in an emergency and your records show a different type.

6 Keep an eye out for clues. Check bank statements and your and your children's records regularly. Take note if any official mail doesn't arrive at its destination. You have a limited amount of time to report fraud – if you don't catch it in time, there may not be a way to undo the damage.

26 HOW TO SURVIVE A JOB INTERVIEW

After months of searching, you've finally found a job you want and have made it through to the interview stage. Bravo. Now comes the tricky part – you have to sell yourself, without appearing to be a sell-out.

1 Do your research and find out about the company you are hoping to join, and be ready to explain why you want to work there and what you can bring to the table.

2 Don't *say* you're a people person – *act* like one. Avoid playing the quirky card; make yourself seem like someone who would be easy to work with. Interviews are often just a way to find out how well you'll fit in.

3 Build rapport before boasting. In the beginning of an interview, be sure it's a fifty-fifty exchange between you and them. After that, it's OK if you're doing most of the talking.

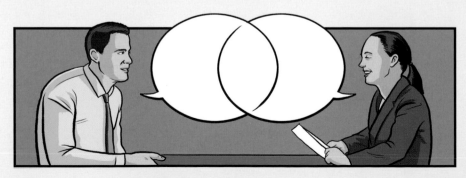

4 Don't dress to impress, dress to fit in. You want to wear something that's a notch more formal than what employees of that company wear to work every day.

5 Sell the story of yourself. The new style of interviewing is to ask candidates to talk about examples of tricky situations they handled well. Prepare for this by having real-life anecdotes ready, but perhaps keep quiet about that time you got drunk and insulted your boss...

6 Spin your weaknesses the right way. Saying you're too much of a perfectionist is amateur and interviewers see right through it. Instead, be honest but focus on things you have actually worked on to improve.

7 Never mention bad blood. Don't speak ill of an old boss or company. Instead, explain that you learned all you could there. It's understood that you may not use your former employer as a reference since job-hunts are often kept confidential.

8 Don't bring up money until there's a good chance you have the job in the bag, or the door opens to discuss a start date. Even then, first enquire about your exact responsibilities and with whom you will be working. One tactic for figuring out where you stand is to ask what the *range* of salaries is for others in your position.

9 Practise. Do a simulated interview with a friend to discover whether you use too many 'um's, don't share enough about yourself or come across as being boring. Video it so you can play back the dummy run and critique your own performance.

10 Ask some questions of your own. Interviewers always offer you the chance to make enquiries and this is another chance to present yourself as someone who will fit in. Ask them what it's like to work there and to work on their team.

11 Wow them with a workfolio. Résumés have gone hi-tech and you can use personal sites that introduce you and highlight your greatest hits in a dynamic way. Some companies prefer the simplicity of a traditional one-page CV, but a workfolio can be an impressive complement.

HOW TO SURVIVE A
WARDROBE MALFUNCTION

Whether it's splitting your skirt on the day of a job interview, missing your mouth and tipping coffee down your front or getting your zip stuck at half mast, there is nothing more painful both socially and physically than a full-blown wardrobe mishap. Thankfully, we're here to help.

1 Do a test run. It is advisable to work out if your chosen get-up can stand the stresses of the day before you leave the house. Do a lunge, a squat, cross and un-cross your legs and test the zip. Prevention is as good as a cure, and all that.

2 Carry these three things with you to any high-stakes event: safety pins (for when a button pops off), superglue (for broken heels, split soles or tears in clothing) and that mini sewing kit you stole from a hotel last year. Avoid tit-tape at all costs.

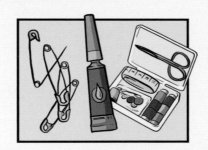

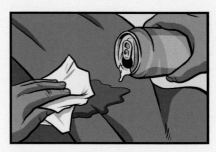

3 Soda water removes stains better than warm or cold tap water. Never rub. Only ever blot. Also, breathe. Clothes can sense panic like dogs can.

4 If you spill water on silk, put that paper napkin *down*. Instead, use a dry piece of the same material to blot up the blotch (if you happen to have a spare bit of dry silk to hand, that is).

5 Halfway to that meeting and realised you've still got the price stickers on the bottom of your new shoes? Don't waste time trying to pick them off. Grab a permanent felt-tipped pen and colour them in so they don't show.

6 Lead pencils are like WD40 to stuck zips. Use the tip of one to loosen the teeth if your fly malfunctions. Just make sure you don't get the pencil jammed in there too. That could be *really* awkward.

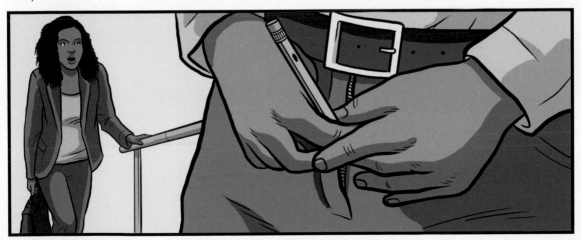

HOW TO SURVIVE
28 BEING MUGGED

The bane of sightseers everywhere, muggings often happen when you're disorientated in an unfamiliar city or part of a crowd. Here are a few tips to outwit crafty crooks.

1 Create a decoy wallet. If you plan on visiting a city with a particularly high robbery rate, carry a sacrificial wallet containing a little cash, an out-of-date ID and an expired credit card. If you do find yourself confronted by a robber, try relinquishing a wad of cash and hope they just run away. But, if they do ask for your wallet or phone, give it up.

2 Know exactly where you're going at all times. Do your revision so you don't drift around a station looking lost or stray into dodgy areas of town. You should also never talk on your phone, wear earphones or flash your tech while in an isolated area – it's a sign to Apple-pickers and iCriminals everywhere that you are a bountiful target.

3 Look confident. Scientists have identified the most effective body language for warding off a would-be mugger: walk fast and tall, taking long strides, turning your pelvis with each step to move your whole body.

4 Don't fall into the distraction trap. If you're in a crowd and you get a shove or someone approaches aggressively in front of you, it's very possible you're being pickpocketed by an accomplice.

5 Make a mental note of what your mugger looks like. You'll need to describe them to the police to stand any chance of getting your stuff back. Then call the cops immediately – robbers are often found nearby or are already known to the authorities.

6 Fill out a police report. Credit-card companies and insurers require official confirmation of the crime before they will cough up.

HOW TO SURVIVE
29 DRESS-DOWN (CASUAL) FRIDAY

You can thank Hawaii for the existence of dress-down Friday. In the 1960s, Hawaiian-shirt manufacturers invented 'Aloha Friday' to stimulate sales and, like all great traditions, it took over the world shortly after.

1 Think smart, not sloppy. Dress-down Friday is about dialling it back a half step from what you normally wear to work; *not* about cranking it up a notch from what you wear watching football on Sunday. It's also not about flashing your crotch or cleavage. The strumpet look is never ideal for work, unless that is your line of business...

2 Fit fixes everything. Slimmer, fitted shirts and pants make even the most casual outfits look more formal. The better the fit, the more you can get away with – although you should perhaps leave the skin-tight PVC catsuit in the bedroom.

3 The more senior you are, the less freedom you have to jazz it up – you still need to be the best-dressed person in the room if you want to be able to exert any authority whatsoever.

4 Mix it up. Very casual pieces such as T-shirts or sweatshirts are OK as long as you combine them with more formal items. Try a blazer over your favourite T-shirt or an Oxford button-down shirt underneath a sweatshirt.

5 Some sports shoes are OK. These have made a comeback in the fashion world, which means they can be paired with anything from a suit to jeans and a T-shirt. Rubber-soled shoes work, too, as long as they're classic and stylish. They should also be clean, not full of holes and without the rather unpalatable cheesy scent that can cling to some footwear.

HOW TO SURVIVE A

30 FAILED PARACHUTE

Parachute malfunctions occur pretty often, about once every 30–40 jumps. These are usually caused by a line twist. Fortunately, this is fairly easy to correct if you stay calm and kick like hell.

1 A safe jump starts with a well-packed chute. Newbies always get a pre-packed rig, while more experienced skydivers – those with a dozen jumps under their belt – have the option of packing their own. However, unless you're skydiving several times a month, it's best to leave it to the experts.

2 Once you've exited the plane, your freefall body position is the key to a clean chute deployment. Anything other than a horizontal belly-to-earth pose increases your chances of a snag or twist. If you're not in the right position, arch your back and your body will usually correct itself.

3 Once you've pulled your main chute, look up to make sure it has fully deployed. If not, don't panic. First, look at the direction of the twist, then shake or kick out of it by swinging your legs in the opposite direction. The more severe the twist, the more violent the kicking needs to be. Nine out of 10 times the chute will untwist.

4 By 762m (2500ft), it's vital (literally) that you have a full deployment – you're dropping at roughly 90m (300ft) per second... If not, it's time to release the main chute from your rig and pull your reserve chute. Immediately look up and check for twists.

5 If the reserve chute is twisted, don't stop kicking – your goal is to create as much drag as possible and those who survive have always somehow managed to open their chute just enough to catch some air and slow their plummet. Alive and kicking is a truism in this scenario...

HOW TO SURVIVE
31 THE FIRST WEEK OF COLLEGE

Many people say their first week of college was one of the most exciting, frightening and overwhelming of their lives – those who were sober enough to remember it, anyway...

1 Go it alone. People who arrive at college hankering after a girlfriend or boyfriend back home tend to isolate themselves and are less likely to make the effort to find new friends.

2 Keep an open-door policy. From the day you move into your new digs, leave your door open as often as possible so passers-by know you're interested in meeting new people.

3 Beat the bookstore rush. Order all your books online and have them delivered directly to your door. Better yet, see which ones are available for download on your tablet.

4 Do a campus dry run. Knowing where a lecture hall is on a map is not enough to ensure you'll get to class on time. Expect it to take longer than you think, for the map to be incorrect, or to find a sign on the door telling you that your class has been moved to a different lecture theatre across campus.

5 Try to remember to drink some water along with all the shots. By all means, enjoy a drink or five, but beware of running yourself ragged and having to miss classes because you're sick. And avoid any 'games' that involve fire, drinking various substances (use your imagination) from shoes or stealing (sorry, 'borrowing') things.

6 Fast food = fast flab. Late-night pizza, post-boozing kebabs and cheap high-carb campus food will take you from a size medium to large before you know it. Try to eat as healthily as you can and consider popping a multivitamin along with the headache pill every morning.

HOW TO SURVIVE AN
ALL-YOU-CAN-EAT BUFFET

Often derided as being uncivilised, all-you-can-eat buffets are a godsend for students, carb-loading athletes and gluttons (sorry, 'gourmands'). Successfully stuffing your face does, however, require a strategy, so here's how to pick your way through the minefield that is dining's most debauched tradition.

1 Don't starve yourself beforehand. People often think that the hungrier they are, the more they will be able to eat. Wrong! Being hungry causes your stomach to shrink and you to fill up faster. Instead, eat a light meal several hours prior to the binge.

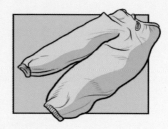

3 Wear sweatpants. They are comfortable, adaptable and it doesn't matter if you drop stuff on them...

2 Go at lunchtime. It will probably be cheaper and it is also best to have your heaviest meal in the middle of the day so you can digest it before you go to bed. Plus you probably won't need any dinner, saving you yet more dosh.

4 Stick to water. All-you-can-eat joints often jack up the price of drinks to make up for money lost on food, and anything carbonated will just make you feel fuller faster. Water, on the other hand, aids digestion.

5 Take a dry run. Survey the buffet without putting a single morsel on your plate – you're looking for the most expensive food (seafood and meat), as well as variety and things you like. For round one, go for a tiny quantity of every item that appeals to you; wait until round two to major on your favourites. Avoid carbs, which are too filling *and* have a low value-per-ounce ratio.

6 You're never too full to eat fruit. Because of its high water content, it won't add to that stuffed feeling. It is also one of the more valuable items at a buffet. Kerching!

HOW TO SURVIVE
33 LAS VEGAS

Whether you want to see your first Picasso, learn about wine from a renowned sommelier or see a world-famous Broadway show, you can get it all and much much more in the heady destination that is Las Vegas.

2 Pace yourself. On the first night, go to a lounge instead of a club – there's usually no cover charge and they have a mellower vibe – perfect for easing into the weekend.

1 Pick the right time to visit. Never book a trip to Vegas while there's a convention in town (you can get this information at www.lvcva.com), as prices will be sky-high. It's a good idea to check that the show, band or magician you have set your heart on seeing will be on offer during your stay.

3 Gamble! A lot of people are too intimidated to grab a chair at a card table. Few realise that most casinos offer free gambling lessons. Remember, if you stick to a predetermined budget you're never losing, you're just paying for a great time – money spent gambling is the cost of admission.

4 Choose your table carefully. Blackjack is by far the most straightforward game, whereas craps is the most complex. Whatever game you choose to play, know your limit. Decide how much you can afford to spend on gambling *before* you arrive and stick to it.

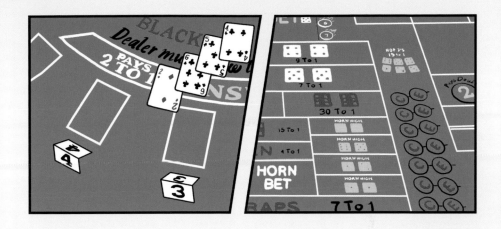

5 Blow your winnings on an amazing meal. Some of the best chefs in the world have restaurants in Las Vegas. Dinner for two will possibly cost the same as your hotel room, but consider when you'll next be in a city where one of these greats has an eatery and how much it would set you back to make a special trip. When in Rome...

6 Get out of town. Rent a car and head toward some of America's most beautiful stretches of wilderness: the Grand Canyon is a four-hour drive away (or a 45-minute helicopter ride); Zion National Park is only two hours' away; and Red Rocks Canyon is just 45 minutes from Vegas.

7 Book a spa treatment. Think of it as essential maintenance, not indulgence. There's no better way to set yourself up for a wild Saturday night than pampering yourself a bit and working off the excesses of the night before.

8 Visit the real Las Vegas. Downtown Vegas, once the stomping ground of the Rat Pack, has been transformed in recent years with chic-but-low-key bars and restaurants. The casinos are also much less intimidating here than on the Strip, and Freemont Street is home to the coolest old-school neon signs in town.

9 Bag the ultimate photo... a selfie of you standing in front of the iconic Las Vegas sign, one block south of Mandalay Bay casino.

34 HOW TO SURVIVE HEARTBREAK

Psychologists say that the key to curing heartbreak is to maintain some control over the things you *can* influence. So pick yourself up, dust yourself off and follow a few simple ground rules.

1 Assess whether or not it's final. Hint: it is. Most relationship breakdowns that result in a break-up are symptomatic of some fairly big issues. Even if you do patch things up, the writing is on the wall.

2 Cry it out. Stock up on comfort food and bad movies. Mourning is part of the process and is much better than distracting yourself from the pain.

3 Take some responsibility. If someone tells you 'it's not you, it's me', understand that it *is* actually partly you. Conversely, if someone places *all* the blame on you for a break-up, it is almost certainly *not* all your fault.

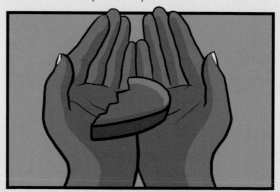

4 Build your force field. Be strict and disciplined about how much contact you have with your ex (none); how often you go to places where you know he or she will be (never); and deciding whether one last fling will help with closure (it won't).

5 Swap social media for being plain social. Things like Facebook force you to maintain involvement in your ex's life. Drop off the social-media map and, instead, meet up with people who represent what your future social life looks like, instead of your past one.

6 Stay single for at least six months. It's better to close yourself off completely for several months than to risk the rebound effect. And count yourself lucky. Break-ups feel like an end, but the search for a soulmate doesn't begin until the day you say goodbye to someone who isn't right for you.

HOW TO SURVIVE A
35 ROAD TRIP

As air travel becomes almost insufferable, consider the art of the road trip. It's classic adventure, nostalgia and awful food all rolled into one.

1 Give your car to a little pre-trip TLC. After your mechanic has given your wheels the once-over, sign up for roadside breakdown cover, hide at least one spare key on the vehicle somewhere, then give it a good clean – your car is not only going to get you from A to B, it's your new living room.

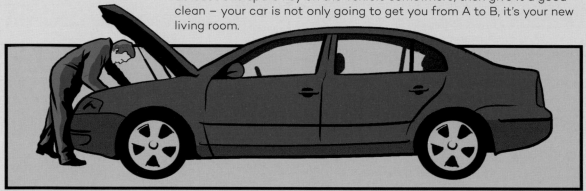

2 Plan (at least a little). While road trips bring out your inner freewheelin', devil-may-care Easy Rider, a little planning will ensure that you hit the most beautiful part of the drive during daylight hours (or, better yet, sunset), and never get stuck in a metro area during rush hour.

3 Become a tech head. There are numerous great sites which plot your route and include info on food, scenic highlights and curious detours. Location-specific apps such as Road Ninja flag up every 'gas/food' exit on your route.

4 Pack a hunger-emergency kit. Hours can pass without any option other than gas-station hot dogs. Pack some real food — trail mix, apples, peanut butter — and plenty of water. And don't forget beer or wine for when you pull into that campsite late at night.

5 Sign up for satellite radio. Most gritty local radio stations have been bought up by multinational corporations anyway, and satellite radio gives you access to a greater variety of tunes, a stronger signal and local traffic updates.

6 Beware of 'scenic' detours. Not all back roads are prettier than the highway. Many actual scenic routes are marked on maps and GPS, so only leave main roads if you're sure it is safe and will be worth it.

HOW TO SURVIVE AN
36 ALL-NIGHTER

The last time you stayed awake all night you were probably being either incredibly responsible (studying for a test) or incredibly irresponsible (at a never-ending party). Our advice? If you have to do the former, be sure to celebrate with the latter.

1 Pay off all your sleep debt. If you haven't had at least one great night's sleep going into your all-nighter – preferably a few nights – it will be extremely difficult to go the distance.

2 Stock up on anti-sleep supplies. First, pick a stimulant: coffee contains about 80mg of caffeine, whereas some energy drinks and over-the-counter pills have up to 200mg. Taurine and vitamin B are natural options.

3 Use booze wisely. Alcohol has a stimulating effect initially, but get ready for the downer stage once you've hit your limit. If heavy drinking is involved in your all-nighter, take a long break from the booze at some point and then pick back up again as morning approaches.

4 Walk towards the light. Our natural sleep hormone stops being produced when we're in bright, especially blue-wavelength, light. Even the glow generated by TV, computer and smartphone screens is said to keep us awake so if you're flagging in a dark club, spend some time looking at your phone.

5 Take a power nap if possible. This should be no less than 20 minutes and no more than an hour – if you enter REM sleep, you may never recover. If possible, take another nap around 5am, which is when you're likely to feel most tired.

6 Take a walk around the block. Sitting upright – or even working standing up – and any activity that gets the blood flowing will help stave off sleepiness.

37 HOW TO SURVIVE A GUNSHOT WOUND

Being shot is never fun. The good news, however, is that if you are hit by a 'stray' bullet, this will probably have come from a handgun and be less damaging than a rifle round. If you're also lucky enough to receive a soft-tissue wound and are not bleeding much, you may be able to get yourself to safety or a hospital. In general, though, it is best to avoid being shot in the first place...

1 Avoid war zones and post offices – in a battlefield or disgruntled-employee situation, you're more likely to be threatened by a high-velocity firearm, such as a hunting or assault rifle. This can break bones, puncture lungs and sever arteries, even if the shot isn't a direct hit.

2 Want to avoid being shot altogether? Move to Japan: it has the lowest incidence of gun violence for a developed country (about 10 gun homicides per year).

3 Mug up on the US military acronym M.A.R.C.H.: Massive hemorrhaging, Airway, Respiration, Circulation, and Hyper- or Hypothermia – in that order. If you have to treat a shooting victim, cover any chest wounds; make sure the airway is open (lying down isn't always the best position); check for good respiration; that blood is circulating well; that the victim isn't too cold or too hot.

4 Bleeding out is your biggest concern. Applying pressure is key but a tourniquet may be even better. Create a 5cm-wide (2in-wide) strip of fabric (a narrower one can cause permanent damage; a wider one is ineffective) and tie it 5cm (2in) above the wound.

5 Get to a hospital!

HOW TO SURVIVE
38 LOCKING YOURSELF OUT OF YOUR HOTEL ROOM NAKED

You always thought it could only happen to Mr Bean, but here you are, stark naked, locked out of your own hotel room. In Vegas, this scenario is as routine as forgetting your credit card behind the bar. Everywhere else, it could land you in jail.

1 Cover your pink bits. The fine line between fully nude and ever-so-slightly covered could be the difference between hilarity and handcuffs.

2 Scan the hallway around you for the two things that are often sitting right outside hotel rooms: room-service napkins and newspapers. In a pinch, a potted plant will do the trick.

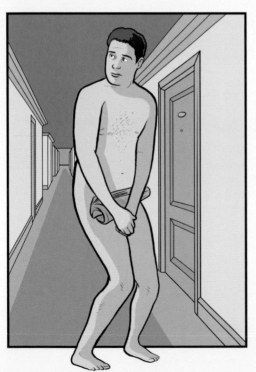

3 Sheepishly knock on your neighbour's door and come up with an opening line that won't freak them out the minute they look through the peephole. Ask for a towel or robe and for them to kindly call reception for you.

4 Find the maid's closet. It may require a little frantic searching, but you'll then have all the sheets and towels you could dream of and can drape yourself, toga-style, with fetching white linen.

5 Stay out of the lobby. This is the most crowded and conspicuous place you can possibly go. Find a phone and call for help rather than presenting your wares to the night staff at the front desk.

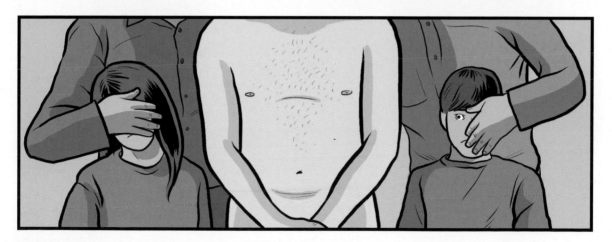

6 If you have to venture away from your floor, take the stairs. It may be a pain, but it's better than trapping some poor unsuspecting family in the elevator and trying to make casual conversation.

HOW TO SURVIVE A
39 ZOMBIE ATTACK

Flesh-eating, brain-dead and highly infectious, zombies can ruin your day. They infect through any exchange of fluids, so protection is key.

1 Get some body armour. Chain mail is ideal but hard to find. Look for chainsaw-rated gear at your local DIY store. Underneath, wear an all-in-one protective suit and get a good dust mask and goggles.

2 If you are bitten, immediately tourniquet the limb tightly. Encourage it to bleed by keeping it low and very warm, to discourage clotting. If the flesh looks as though it has been infected, amputate immediately.

3 Use neat bleach to clean up any liquids that come from zombies. At 5 per cent sodium hypochlorite, it is strong enough to kill most viruses and bacteria.

4 Travel at the sunniest, hottest times Zombies are unlikely to have the same cooling responses as humans, and moving generates heat in their bodies. Even if they can withstand the pain of hyperthermia, there is a maximum load their body can take; they may literally have a meltdown.

5 If a zombie does not display the full spectrum of symptoms, herd immunity may be starting. Isolate them to confirm this is not just delayed-onset zombification. If it is real, take a blood sample and wait for it to clot in a sterile dish. The lighter, runny liquid that separates from the clot may contain valuable antibodies. Find a volunteer for trials.

6 Once the epidemic infects 30 per cent of the population it will be unstoppable, but if it is biological (rather than supernatural) you can wait it out. Basic maths tells us that a sedentary, unfed 80kg (175lb) zombie will waste away to a pile of bones and skin after 150 days. Stockpile enough supplies for five or six months, and stay indoors.

HOW TO SURVIVE
40 WAKING UP WITH A NEW TATTOO

Sobered up to discover a random 'ancient' symbol or your partner/child/dog's name etched on your skin? Wish you'd thought twice before braving the tattooist's bench and succumbing to some dermatological graffiti? Yes? Here's what to do if you wake up sporting an ill-advised yin-yang...

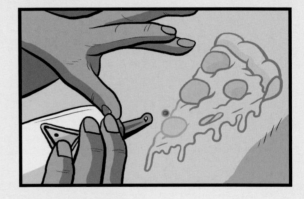

1 Keep it clean and covered. Use antibacterial wash and sterile dressings to cover the fresh tattoo, which will probably still be weeping fluids.

2 Do you want it? If so, great. If not, you need to speak to a dermatologist about removal. Creams and dermabrasion are not as successful as laser removal, which agitates the pigments under the skin to break them up.

3 The removal process will depend on many factors. The size of the tattoo, the colour of your skin and the pigments used in the ink will all affect how many sessions of laser treatment you'll need. Darker skin is problematic because it can lighten afterwards: you may want to consider changing the tattoo to a design you like instead.

4 Check the pigments in your tattoo. If possible, ask the tattooist for the exact shade and brand they use. Generally, darker tones such as black, blue and red are easier to remove than brighter ones, such as yellow, purple and pink. Green is usually the hardest to remove.

5 You may need as many as 10 treatments, with at least four weeks between each one, to remove the tattoo. Your skin will need breaks to heal and naturally dispose of the broken-up pigments. Tattoo in haste, repent at leisure...

6 Use a high-factor sunblock on your tattoo every day during the removal process. Painkillers may help with the soreness after your removal sessions, but they won't take away the regret.

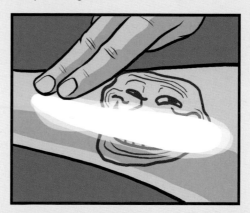

HOW TO SURVIVE AN
41 AVALANCHE

There are plenty of smart things you can do to avoid an avalanche altogether: check the local avalanche forecast, steer clear of areas where you can see that other avalanches have occurred, and stay away from slopes with 28- to 38-degree aspects, among other things. But if you simply can't resist a bit of fresh powder, be prepared.

1 Before setting out on foot or skis on a suspect slope, make sure you're wearing an avalanche beacon, which will transmit a signal to rescuers if you are buried.

2 As you venture on to the surface of the slope, remove your hands from the straps on your ski poles (poles and skis act as anchors in the event of a slide). If there are several of you in a group, ski or walk the area one at a time so that if you do get caught, there are others free to rescue you.

3 If you hear a 'whump!', brace yourself. The first signs of a slide are the sound and feel of the snow settling – or dropping – all at once. You now have a matter of seconds to ski or run across the slope to the outside edge, where the snow is usually not moving as quickly, giving you a better chance of reaching safety.

4 If there's no time to get out of the way, make your body as big as possible and swim for your life. Like when you shake a can of mixed nuts and the larger Brazil nuts rise to the top, you want to become an object that will come to the surface of the slide rather than sinking to the bottom.

5 Thirty per cent of people who perish in avalanches die from being crushed by blocks of snow as large as refrigerators, or from being thrown over cliffs or into rocks and trees. If you happen to survive the gauntlet of obstacles, do whatever you can to keep any part of your body or clothing above the snow so that rescuers will be able to spot you.

6 Try to put a hand or arm in front of your face before you come to a full stop, in order to create an air pocket. Resist the urge to struggle or dig yourself out of the snow – avalanche debris settles like cement. Instead, remain calm and preserve your oxygen with slow, steady breathing.

7 If you have managed to mark your location, you could be recovered in whatever time it takes to simply dig you out. If rescuers can't see you, but you're wearing a transmitting beacon, it could take up to 20 minutes to reach you. If rescuers have no idea of where you're buried, there's no telling. Either way, you only have about 15–20 minutes of air. Even though snow is full of oxygen, ice will form around your warm breath and form what avalanche nerds call a 'death mask'. Nice.

HOW TO SURVIVE A
42 NETWORKING EVENT

Work-related events can be excruciating, embarrassing and boring for most, but some people seem to know the secret of making networking actually pay. Be that person.

1 Create a clear list of target connections beforehand. Decide what the best, OK and worst scenarios will be in terms of sheer numbers of people with whom you have contact: promise yourself you can leave when you hit the top target.

2 Don't be the first to arrive. Be there when the event starts getting interesting, because you'll enjoy it more and will spend less time having to talk to strangers.

3 It's a two-drink night, max: non-drinkers will be watching you and judging constantly. Don't get lumbered with loud, drunk people – the pros find these types toxic.

4 Don't be the clown. The more you try with people the less you actually impress them – and they probably don't want to be there either. Use 'soft' eye contact, looking around their face rather than glaring into their pupils like a hypnotist.

5 Instead of asking all the questions, tell people about yourself. By giving people your take on events or the way you experienced a similar episode to them, you'll come across as more human and draw them closer.

6 Don't bring reams of paperwork to give out because it will stop people needing to give you their details. Never be the last to leave. You'll be stuck with the drunks and no-hopers who are there to get smashed and who probably haven't made any connections all night.

43

HOW TO SURVIVE A MIDLIFE CRISIS

Stand-up advice to avoid your own downfall. Read on to learn how to grow old gracefully. Well, without becoming a total cliché, at any rate.

1 Don't assume you're immune. It doesn't matter how old you are – as careers peak earlier and people marry later, midlife crises can happen as early as your late thirties. Plenty of people feel stressed, useless, lonely and washed-up by this stage – the prerequisites of early-onset MLC. If you recognise these emotions, take action.

2 Do something scary. Is your life too 'safe' and 'boring'? Staying within your comfort zone means you're less likely to face negative emotions. By taking small risks and being more spontaneous – starting with little things like trying a new gym class or going to the cinema on your own – you'll automatically feel excited, braver and more present in your life.

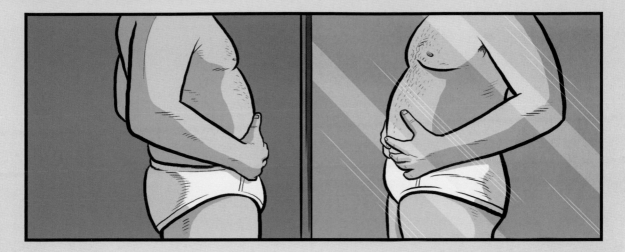

3 Don't have an affair. Yes, your partner isn't quite as stunning as they were when you first met them in the flush of youth – but have you looked in the mirror at yourself recently? The answer to a midlife crisis lies with you, not with somebody else.

4 Invest in a bicycle, not a sports car. They're cool again – and much better for you physically and mentally. Exercising outdoors is a proven mood-booster, stimulating all your senses and, in turn, your mind. It's also a lot cheaper than that convertible you think you want.

5 Take a spoonful of German medicine. *Schadenfreude* can be extremely effective medication for a midlife crisis. Hate your job? Think about people sweeping the streets. Hate your house? Think about people struggling to get on the property ladder. Hate your tattoo? See page 106...

6 Unplug at weekends. Stress is the time-honoured chauffeur of the MLC, and there's nothing more guaranteed to drive you round the bend than constant emails or work phone calls when you need to recharge. Digitally detox at weekends (see page 214) and reap the mental rewards of silence.

7 Edit your friendship list. It's OK to cull people who don't help you grow. Friendships should be enriching, not draining. It's time to reassess some of those numbers you never call.

8 Spend time with your own parents. Because you understand them better now, and because they won't be around for much longer. As a bonus, there's nothing more guaranteed to make you feel younger.

9 Do one thing mindfully each day. Mindfulness is an easy way to ground yourself in the present and get out of your own head. Employ all five senses on one task daily: something you'd normally do on autopilot. For example, if you're eating, what does the food look like, feel like, smell like? What does that first bite taste like? Flicking this simple switch will instantly relax you – and make your life more vivid and enjoyable.

44

HOW TO SURVIVE A
KNOCKOUT PUNCH

Your opponent's winding up a haymaker and you've got a precious split second to save yourself: whether you're in a bar or the boxing ring, how do you avoid the KO?

1 Bring both of your fists up to your face. Clench your knuckles as tightly as possible, with each fist touching its respective cheek. The tighter against your face the better, as this will diffuse the blow. Tuck your elbows in to keep your guard as solid as possible.

2 Close your mouth. It's possibly what got you into trouble in the first place, but right now it needs to be shut – tight. If your mouth is open when you get hit, it could lead to a broken jaw or teeth.

3 Keep your chin down. This reduces the amount of face exposed as a target – and the distance your head will fly back when taking the punch. If you are hit on your forehead rather than your jaw or chin, it reduces your chances of being knocked out.

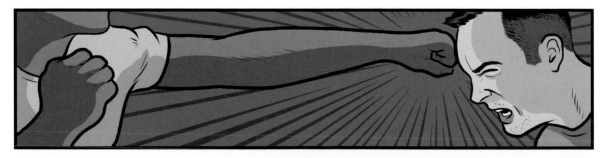

4 Maintain eye contact with your attacker. If you can't see them, you can't predict the angle of their shot or watch for weaknesses to exploit on your counter-attack. It's natural to want to close your eyes when you see a punch coming, but the impact will feel much more intense if you are blind, making your brain more likely to black out.

5 Roll with the punch. Move your body or head in the direction of the blow. This decreases the power in the shot, giving it less impact and you more leverage to come back with a counter-punch.

6 Fight back, if you are in a boxing match; otherwise, perhaps make yourself scarce before the cops turn up.

HOW TO SURVIVE

The dreaded words 'you're fired' still ringing in your ears, you've done the walk of shame with your cardboard box crammed with paperclips and a half-dead pot plant, and now you're out in the big bad world of the job market. What to do?

1 Get a second opinion about your dismissal. Depending on the circumstances, it can be useful to speak to a lawyer or a union. 'Wrongful termination' does happen and there are laws to protect workers. Listen carefully to what the Human Resources department says and know your rights.

2 Check what you're entitled to in the way of support. If redundancy is being offered, the amount will typically be dependent on the length of time served. If you receive a payout, bank it, don't spend it on whisky. Analyse your expenditure and work out where you can cut back in the short term while maintaining essential payments (mortgage, schooling, insurance, credit cards, not whisky).

3 Update your résumé and LinkedIn profile. Reach out to your network of contacts – you *have* been maintaining your contacts, haven't you? Update your recommendations, references and photos. Follow potential employers on social media so you get wind of vacancies or projects that suit your skills.

4 Consider retraining. Perhaps this is the right time to do something completely different? There may be grants available to help you change career or set up a business.

5 Let yourself grieve. You may have really, *really* liked your former colleagues and your job. It's OK to feel sad. Talk to others and share the pain. Then put your best foot forwards.

HOW TO SURVIVE
46 FALLING THROUGH ICE

When ice starts cracking beneath you, it's too late to regret not knowing the difference between stronger clear ice and weaker white ice. You're going in, like it or not.

1 Once you take the icy plunge, control your breathing immediately. The shock of the cold will cause you to expel all the air in your lungs in a gasp – drowning is a very real threat in these first few seconds.

2 Shout for help. Now is the time to test out how loud you really can holler.

3 Shed anything that is going to weigh you down or hinder your escape, such as backpacks and skis. Insulated clothing can add buoyancy and warmth so keep these on. Keep any sharp tools to hand too.

4 Decide on the best exit point – typically this will be the point where you fell through the ice. Ice must have a minimum thickness of 10cm (4in) in order to support a human's weight. Prepare to put every shred of effort into getting out; don't conserve energy – it's all or nothing. Your muscles will become too cold to function after a few minutes in the water.

5 To get out of the water, exit horizontally, like a seal, spreading your weight over the ice and kicking hard. If you have sharp tools, jab them into the ice for leverage. Roll away from the hole before sliding along the ice or crawling, evenly distributing your mass. You can't afford to get a second dunking in the icy water.

6 When you're back on land or safe ice, seek help and shelter pronto. Get warm; you have an hour before severe hypothermia sets in. Good luck!

HOW TO SURVIVE A
47 PHALL CURRY

A phall curry is so hot it's off the menu. Many contain explosive scorpion or naga chillies, which scorch in at over two million on the Scoville scale of heat. That's hotter than a gas bomb. How the hell are you going to defuse this one?

1 Build tolerance. It takes years of practice and burnt taste buds, but you can increase your curry resistance. Just do so carefully: people have been hospitalised during curry-eating competitions. The Scoville scale – a measurement of chilli heat – is a good series of benchmarks to slowly ascend.

2 Request separate sauce. Many restaurants now serve this as standard, but even if they don't, they'll happily oblige if you ask. This allows you to try before you die (not literally) – and control the edible lava's flow over your meat.

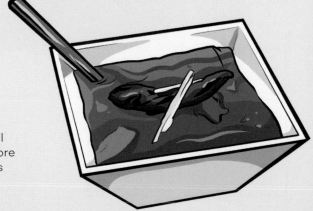

3 Drink milk, not water. That infernal fire on your tongue is caused by a specific ingredient: the capsaicin in the chilli. The good news is that there's a specific counteragent too: casein. This is found in milk and yoghurt, so it's a pint of the white stuff for you. It work bests if you drink it before tucking in.

4 Order a tactical side dish. In this scenario, a casein-rich cucumber or mint raita is in order – think of it as a handy fire extinguisher at your side. Sadly, there isn't a naan on the planet that will help break your phall...

5 Sugar your spice. A spoonful of sugar can help more than the medicine go down. It assists by absorbing the spicy oil coating in your mouth, as well as giving your taste buds a stronger sensation to concentrate on.

6 Lassi but not least. Down this creamy Indian dessert drink, which is a potent combination of sugar and dairy – a knockout one-two for any capsaicin still lingering on your tongue.

HOW TO SURVIVE
48 WRITER'S BLOCK

Still staring at that blank page? Overcoming writer's block is like navigating a roadblock: easy to get around if you know some shortcuts.

1 Pour a glass of red. Just one, obviously, but a tot of red wine can dramatically improve your creative powers. The secret lies in a part of your brain called the anterior cingulate cortex, which controls both task performance and emotions. If you can relax this – which a little red will do – the Alpha brainwaves will flow, and so will the words.

2 Embrace the 'adjacent possibles'. In other words, go for a short walk. Exposing your brain to new shapes, colours and smells will spark creative juxtapositions that will feed and unblock your brain.

3 Use a mind map to redirect your thinking. Take a piece of A3 paper, write your central concept in the middle, then everything else that pops into your head around it. Once your brain dump is complete, you can map a path through it.

4 Banish perfectionism. Impossibly high standards are often to blame for writer's block. Instead, simply start writing anything, even if the first few lines or paragraphs seem awful. Think of it as a new keg of beer. There might be froth at the top, but soon enough the good stuff will start to flow.

5 Talk it through. A colleague sitting next to you, a friend or relative on the phone – it doesn't matter. Explaining a concept to somebody will help you to clarify it in your own mind.

6 Sleep on it. If you leave an idea to ferment while you catch some Zs, it will often hatch itself – usually just before you drift off or immediately after you wake.

HOW TO SURVIVE A
49 STOCK MARKET CRASH

Markets down by 20 per cent recently? It's a crash! Make yourself financially fit by following a few rules and a doing a bit of groundwork so you can survive long enough to turn the catastrophe into a win.

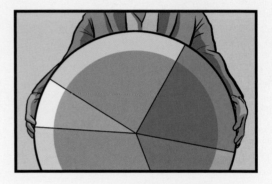

1 Don't invest all your financial eggs in the basket that employs you. In a major crash, there is a chance you'll lose your job and portfolio and end up with, well, egg on your face.

2 Diversify your assets by owning stocks, bonds, cash, commodities and real estate. If one asset class plunges, the others may save you. Keep some cash on the side in case of a severe crash.

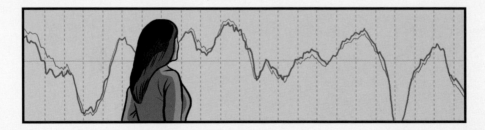

3 Study the moving averages. Before a crash, the major stock indexes will often fall below their moving averages, especially below the 200-day moving average. Also check the sentiment indicators, which will be high before a crash.

4 Be willing to hang on to your cash. There is no rule that says you have to be 100 per cent invested in the stock market, and sometimes watching from the sidelines is the right strategy.

5 Cut your losses at 10 per cent. Otherwise, a small loss can turn into a 30-per-cent disaster. Even if there isn't a crash, selling when you are down 10 per cent still makes sense.

6 If you are down by 30-50 per cent, don't panic. Don't sell everything immediately, because it is possible the market is at rock bottom and will rise.

HOW TO SURVIVE
50 BEING LOST IN THE WILD WITHOUT GPS

While GPS and cell phones make it virtually impossible to get lost these days, who can blame you if you want to leave technology behind when you venture off into the woods. But if you do decide to trust your inner compass, you'd better know what to do if you lose your bearings...

1 Instagram, Twitter, carrier-pigeon – it doesn't matter how you do it, let at least one other person know where you plan on hiking or backpacking *before* you set off. Do this and, if you do get lost, there's a 90 per cent chance you'll be found in the first 24 hours.

2 In order to try to get yourself back on track, stop moving the minute you realise you're lost. If you're like most people who go astray in the wild, you're probably not far from civilisation.

3 Backtracking is the first thing you should try – but it's *essential* that you mark the way with heavy footsteps, pieces of torn clothing or rock markers. Even though you have a hunch about where you came from, you must be able to return to the exact spot at which you first realised you were lost. If backtracking doesn't lead you into more familiar territory, stop, retrace your steps and return to where you started.

4 Based on your energy levels, the weather, and how much daylight you have left, keep doing this until you either pick up a familiar trail or feel you've run out of options. If you're still stumped, return to your original position.

5 Now, you're officially lost and will have to rely on others to find you, so it's essential that you sit tight, in one place. Most people who stay put are found within hours of going missing, but it can take rescuers days to find moving targets, if they find you at all.

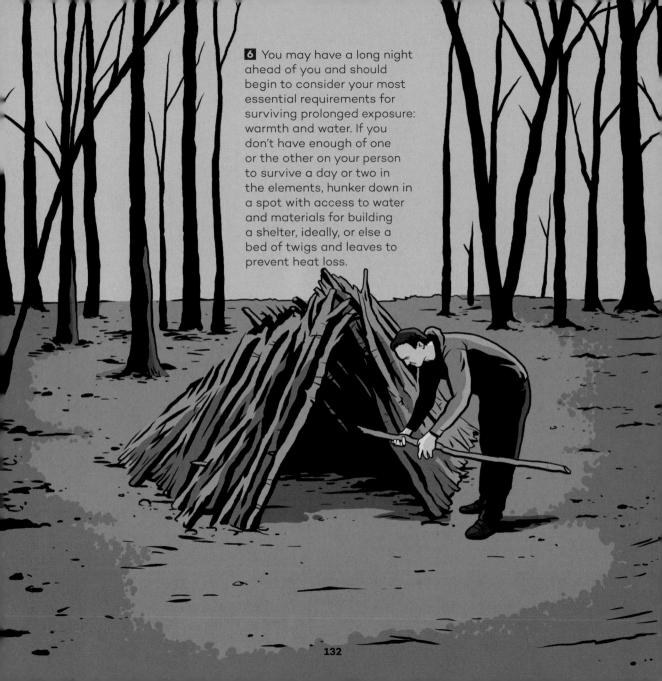

6 You may have a long night ahead of you and should begin to consider your most essential requirements for surviving prolonged exposure: warmth and water. If you don't have enough of one or the other on your person to survive a day or two in the elements, hunker down in a spot with access to water and materials for building a shelter, ideally, or else a bed of twigs and leaves to prevent heat loss.

7 At this stage, it may be time to help yourself, using age-old navigation tools such as the Sun, stars and landscape. Go to the highest vantage point in the area to get the lay of the land and try to spot a road, farm or anything man-made, to determine in which direction you want to begin travelling.

8 One promising lead is water flow: even the smallest stream usually meets up with a river. Traditionally, civilisations have often congregated where water converges, so go with the flow down stream.

9 For simply determining north and south, look to the stars. Polaris, the North Star, is one of the brightest in the sky in the northern hemisphere, while in the southern hemisphere you can use the Southern Cross, the stars Canopus and Achernar or the Magellanic Clouds to help you find the south celestial pole.

10 One of the best methods of determining east and west is to plunge a stick in the ground and another at the edge of its shadow. Wait an hour and place another stick at the edge of the shadow in its new position – the line of sticks grows eastwards as the Sun moves.

HOW TO SURVIVE A
MESSY DIVORCE

Every aspect of divorce is stressful – from divvying up assets to determining custody arrangements and untangling previously entwined lives. So how *do* you survive it?

1 Indulge in the pain. By all means, feel sorry for yourself. Wallowing is a viable strategy – as long as it has a time limit. A good target is a month.

2 Name your emotions. When you feel a strong feeling surfacing, name it. 'Here's the emotion of guilt', 'Here's anxiety again', and so on. This gives you distance from it, and control over it. Picture these emotions as trains pulling into a station. Do you want to jump aboard? No? Then let it leave without you.

3 Keep a diary. Once all of those confused emotions are on a page there won't be so many inside you any more. It's also an excellent means of tracking how far you've come when you look back at this period.

4 Embrace change. The best way to do this is to break routines. Change your commute; change where you have lunch; change the time you wake up in the morning. And start a new hobby – what have you always really wanted to do? Something creative is ideal – a positive, rewarding outlet for all of the anxiety and confusion that comes hand-in-hand with divorce.

6 Always wear good underwear. Self-esteem is important, and this is an easy confidence boost. Plus, you never know...

5 Don't rush back into the fray. If you arrive at the airport with too much baggage, you're going to end up paying for it. The same is true of your next relationship. And there *will* be one.

HOW TO SURVIVE
52 BEING INTERVIEWED ON LIVE TV

It's your 15 minutes of fame! Wait, is that ketchup on your collar? And what did you just say? Oh dear...

1 Slop on the slap. You'll be offered it, so don't be shy. Yes, that means you too, gentlemen: studio lights are harsh and HD cameras are harsher. If you're offered a bit of powder, take it. No one likes a sweaty interviewee: you'll just look nervous and shifty.

2 Chum up with the crew. Woe betide you if you upset the cameraman. The person looking through the lens has all the power. They can make you look great or terrible. So get them a coffee (if the opportunity arises), play nice, and they'll look after you. Ask them how you look. If you've been friendly they won't lie.

3 Speak slowly and clearly. Relax; don't practise too much or lay on the jargon with a shovel. A good trick is to pretend you're explaining something to your grandmother. If she can understand it, most people will.

4 Know your message and get it across. Don't lose sight of why you're there. You must have something interesting to say, or you wouldn't have been asked.

5 Use your hands. We're not talking full French mime artist here, but underlining your point with body language can genuinely help: a moderate amount of hand waving can really get your point across.

6 Expect a curveball. Every interviewer loves one, and it's almost certain to come towards the end of the interview. Just answer quickly, turn it back to what you want to say and carry on. If the interviewer persists just give them a quick verbal jab to the chin – they probably deserve it.

HOW TO SURVIVE AN
53 ULTRAMARATHON

Death and marathons go way back. Legend has it that the original marathoner, Pheidippides, dropped dead after delivering news of victory to Athens. So how do you run even further – an *ultra*marathon – and survive?

1 Set your intention. The most important thing when signing up for any endurance race is to pinpoint exactly *why* you want to do it (masochism? madness?). Knowing that intention will help you maintain commitment and motivation during long hours of training – and the race itself.

2 Choose your footwear carefully. Most ultramarathons are done off-road, so you'll need decent trail-running shoes, suited to your gait. Sort these out from the word go so your feet and ankles get used to them before the race.

3 A solid training plan is crucial. A key component should be back-to-back long training runs. These help your body adapt to 'running tired'. In the last two weeks before the race, you may want to consider tapering slightly so you don't deplete your glycogen stores and your muscles aren't fatigued. Run just as frequently as before, but reduce the length of your runs to keep you ticking over nicely.

4 Loosen your shoelaces on race day. Repetitive impact means your feet will swell over the course of an ultramarathon, so allow for this by cutting your feet some slack.

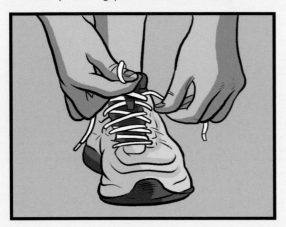

5 Breathe properly. When things start to get hard during the race, focus on your technique. It's easy to take shallow breaths when under stress, but full breathing – using your whole lung capacity – is far more effective.

6 Stay in the moment. Don't overwhelm yourself by thinking about just how far away the finishing line is or how many more kilometres you have to haul ass. Break down the race into sections and only focus on the one you are currently in; literally take it one step at a time.

7 Don't be afraid to take walk-breaks. Match your technique to the terrain: if you're climbing for a long distance then power-walking can be as efficient as running. Equally, if you have long descents, small steps will help you conserve your energy. Often, you'll need to hold some juice in reserve in order to last the distance.

8 Have a mantra. Something simple to repeat over and over to yourself in times of exhaustion. Preferably a simple phrase that epitomises your commitment to the race. For example, Olympic gold-medallist Jessica Ennis-Hill always uses the same mantra: 'Eyes on the prize, eyes on the prize...'

You're taking on water and there's not a desert island in sight. You can swim, right?

1 Always sail with a 'grab bag'. These are waterproof duffel bags containing a radio, satellite phone, sea biscuits, an emergency beacon, compass, flares and seasickness tablets. If the ship goes down, try to also take as much drinking water as you can carry, a hat, a mirror for signalling, any containers you can find for collecting rainwater, and a hook and line for catching fish.

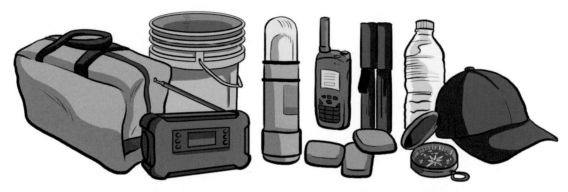

2 Stay with your boat as long as possible. This is because it's bigger than a life raft – and your best chance of being spotted by rescuers.

3 Go drogue. Your priority upon entering the raft is to make sure the drogue – a kind of underwater parachute – is cast out to minimise drift and stop the craft rolling.

4 Keep yourself in good nick. Take your seasickness pills, stay hydrated and reduce your exposure to the sun – ensure your head is covered at all times, ideally by a hat or an item of clothing.

5 Start fishing as quickly as you can. Fish will be attracted by the sinking boat and the underside of your raft as it drifts off, because seaweed and algae will collect there. You'll have to eat them raw, but the good news is that the blood is thirst-quenching.

6 Forget trying to navigate. You'll be taken by the current and where you drift will be out of your hands. The most important thing is not to panic and to concentrate on survival: the reality is that there are a *lot* of ships out there, especially if you're in the North Atlantic. In the meantime, you've got the fish blood to look forward to...

HOW TO SURVIVE
55 TO 100 YEARS OLD

Half of all babies born today will celebrate their 100th birthday. As you're not a baby (unless you're an incredibly literate one), how do you ensure you join them in the 100 club?

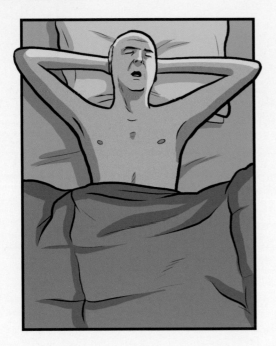

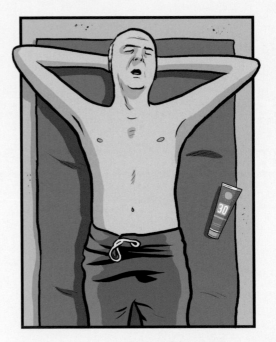

1 Rest more. Want to reach a century? Make sure you spend enough time in the land of nod. Scientists recently discovered that a significant number of centenarians slept for 10 hours or more a night – and had done for much of their adult lives. So swap your raving clobber for some comfy pyjamas, and late-night booze for cups of cocoa.

2 Get into the sunlight. Once you've woken from your epic slumber, get outdoors as quickly as possible. Every minute counts: just one extra hour of sunlight a week can kill cancer cells in your body and prolong your life. Of course this doesn't mean you should burn yourself to a crisp (an open invitation to those cancer cells), but a small amount of sun exposure is vital for health and well-being.

3 Buy a pet. A dog is an excellent excuse to get outdoors every morning – and live to see plenty more. Finnish researchers discovered that looking after an animal helps prolong your life by reducing your blood pressure and safeguarding your heart. Now that's true love.

4 Snack on dried seaweed. That peckish moment mid-morning? Turn to kelp for help. In dried or tablet form, seaweed can reduce your fat absorption rate by up to 75 per cent, keeping your organs fit and healthy.

5 Embrace neurobics. This is the practice of surprising your brain with unexpected actions, providing mental exercise that can keep the grey matter functioning better for longer. Use three or four different routes to return home from work, for example, or brush your teeth with the opposite hand (not necessarily at the same time – you'll get funny looks on the bus).

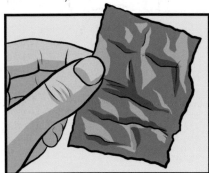

6 Eat real food. If you can't tell what's in it, don't eat it. Fad diets come and go, but the main message is that you should eat a rainbow of fresh foods, avoiding processed ones (especially processed red meat) and enjoy things in moderation. Being overweight ain't going to help you live a long time, so swap the bag of chips for that seaweed we were talking about.

7 Exercise. We are essentially animals, and our bodies are designed to run around rather than slobbing out on a sofa or sitting in front of a computer for hours on end. Find an activity you enjoy and make time to do it regularly.

8 Drink like a Sardinian. The Mediterranean island has a disproportionately large number of centenarians and Italian scientists believe they know why: wine. The rich red stuff produced there contains three times the amount of heart-protecting polyphenols as an average bottle. So celebrate each day with a glass of Sardinian red (yes, just the one) – and toast your own good health.

56 HOW TO SURVIVE JETLAG

Scientists say it's easier to travel west because the body naturally works to a schedule that is slightly longer than 24 hours. Going west extends our day; going east shortens it. But you probably can't avoid heading into the sunset at some point.

1 Get a head start at home. You sleep best in your own bed. If you are going on a long trip, begin to make the transition before you leave, incrementally adjusting to the time zone you will be visiting.

2 Don't take a sleeping pill unless the flight lasts seven hours or more, as it will just make you even drowsier at the other end. If you do take one, choose the most natural option, melatonin.

3 When it comes to sleep, quality is more important than quantity. When you've arrived, drink lots of water, avoid caffeine or alcohol for several hours before bedtime, and recreate the most home-like environment you can with photos, white noise, earplugs or whatever else minimises interruptions.

4 Seek out sunlight. The presence or absence of light is a key cue for your body to know when it should be awake or asleep. During daylight hours, get as much natural light as possible. If you must sleep during the day, go for a black-out in your room.

5 Go for a run. Exercise produces hormones that help regulate energy levels and will speed up the adjustment process. Do not exercise in the hours leading up to bedtime, however, as the adrenalin can make it hard to drop off.

6 Use a jetlag calculator. Enter your current and destination time zones and these handy online tools will let you know the optimum times to sleep and to expose yourself to daylight.

HOW TO SURVIVE A
57 PENALTY SHOOT-OUT

In soccer, penalty shoot-outs are only used to decide important knockout games. Which makes losing them all the more painful. Here are the best ways to avoid that agony...

1 Always go first if you win the coin toss. Statistically, the team taking the first penalty wins 60 per cent of all shoot-outs. (That's because the second team is under greater pressure; they always have to score just to stay in the game.)

2 Do your homework. There are very few truly random penalty-takers. However unpredictable *they* think they are, most strikers fall into patterns you can spot with study.

3 The older the kicker the better. Penalty-taking is stressful. Time and again, more experienced players prove their worth in high-stakes shoot-outs. The early penalty-takers should always be the oldest outfield players on the pitch.

4 Last on, first up. The length of time a player has been on the pitch will affect their success rate from the penalty spot. Those who have played 30 minutes or less are significantly more likely to score a penalty (86.7 per cent) than those who are mentally exhausted after playing the entire match (80 per cent).

5 Aim outside the envelope. Goalkeepers aren't giant octopuses. From their starting position, they have a limited reach: their so-called 'diving envelope'. If you aim beyond that reach, you have a greater chance of success. Is the keeper standing slightly to one side of their goal? Pinpoint the edge of their envelope on the other side.

6 Visualise. Mental imaging can be very powerful in this scenario. Immediately before you begin your run-up, imagine a perfectly placed shot striking the back of the net. Just by doing so, you're raising the odds of it happening.

HOW TO SURVIVE
58 SINGING KARAOKE

Karaoke – Japanese for 'empty orchestra' – rarely involves privacy and an absence of humiliation, despite a proliferation of private 'karaoke boxes' in recent times. Luckily, there are some simple things you can do to avoid looking a complete chump on stage, unless, of course, that is your intention...

1 Work out your ideal playlist in advance. To protect the ears of your fellow drinkers, it's imperative that you pre-select songs you can realistically deliver. When you make your choice, go for a balance of lyric simplicity, a middling vocal range and popularity. Songs with these three essential qualities include:
'Hey Jude' – The Beatles
'Don't Look Back in Anger' – Oasis
'Waterloo' – ABBA
'Born in the U.S.A.' – Bruce Springsteen
'500 Miles' – The Proclaimers
'Like a Virgin' – Madonna

2 Warm up. To get into acceptable voice before you take centre stage, try some simple exercises:

Sirens: Starting at a note you feel comfortable with, repeat a 'ng' sound at progressively higher notes before coming back down to the original note. Breathe slowly. Try expanding the range lower and higher, then repeat with different sounds: lips buzzing, 'ooh' noises or tongue trills.

Messa di voce: Quietly sing the lowest note you can, then gradually increase the volume to a comfortable maximum, before bringing it back down to quiet. Repeat this crescendo and diminuendo throughout your vocal range.

3 Make sure the mic is 5–8cm (2–3in) from your mouth when you are singing, and gradually pull it away when delivering loud and 'belty' notes. The mic should be held tightly to prevent it moving around and affecting the sound. Grasp it in the middle, aiming it horizontally towards your mouth, rather than holding it vertically.

HOW TO SURVIVE A
59 PRISON SENTENCE

The greatest risk in prisons is violence. The murder rate is seven times higher inside than out, and serious assaults occur on an hourly basis. It's essential that you start your sentence well by sorting out your appearance and sticking to a few simple rules.

1 Get a cropped haircut. This will make you look a bit harder and won't make you stand out as a first-timer. It also gives an opponent less to hang on to in a fight, and a crop has the added bonus of manageability if the showers are hit and miss. Fortnightly showers are a real possibility...

2 Buy a pair of decent trainers. A good make and model will set you out as a sensible 'bod'. Cheap, unfashionable or filthy models will cause you to be marked out as a tramp or junkie. Even the prison officers will treat you accordingly: appearance matters.

3 The best way to survive a prison sentence is by keeping your head down and complying with the system. Most people can get through their sentence without confrontations with either the authorities or other prisoners. The important thing is to stay alert and be able to swerve troublesome people, who are often aggressive, violent and mentally ill.

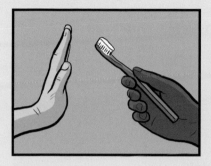

4 There are four unwritten rules you need to follow at all times:

Never borrow anything from another prisoner.
Never reveal the names or addresses of any of your friends or relatives.
Never show fear or weakness.
Keep your relationship with prison staff open and polite, but only speak to them when it is absolutely necessary.

5 Perhaps the best piece of advice is not to wind up in prison in the first place! Crime never pays...

HOW TO SURVIVE

60 RETIREMENT

There are two ways to 'do' retirement. You can lie down and snooze, or you can take action to push the final section of your life to its limits. Getting older should not equate to infirmity, forgetfulness and loneliness – but only you can make the changes.

1 Sleep in every day. Early risers have higher levels of stress hormones and stay angrier right through to the evening, even if they're getting the same total sleep hours as a late-riser. You've earned a lie in.

2 Ditch the car and gadgets and keep moving in every way you can. Walk as much as possible, beat those eggs by hand, chop some wood – it all counts. It may take more time, but hey – what else are you doing?

3 Dance every day. A study of 11 physical activities found that dancing lowers your risk of dementia by 76 per cent. A 21-minute session three times a week is also enough to stave off heart problems, while the physical contact with a dance partner boosts levels of 'feel-good' hormones that will keep you happier.

4 There's no brain-training exercise that has been unequivocally proven to work. Physical exercise, not crosswords, is the thing that will be most effective at staving off dementia.

5 Use a lifetime of accumulated skills for good. Mentor someone, invest in a start-up, get into crowdfunding or set up as a part-time consultant in your field. You dictate the rules and you get the rewards.

6 Give something back. Join a board of governors or become a charity trustee. Feeling embedded in a social group keeps you passionate about what's happening to everyone around you.

HOW TO SURVIVE A
MIGRAINE

'Migraine' – from the Greek words meaning 'half skull' – is a brain disorder that lasts hours or days, and features less-than-fun symptoms including intense pain, nausea, vomiting and oversensitivity to light, noise, smell or motion. These all add up to being something of a headache for sufferers.

1 A migraine is like a faulty alarm that activates pain nerves on the brainstem for no apparent reason. It helps if you can maintain a regular lifestyle pattern, balancing sleep, work and eating.

2 Eat yourself healthy. If you have a migraine, have a fibre-rich breakfast within an hour of getting up. Avoid scoffing too many sugary foods, because the spike and fall in blood glucose can trigger an attack. For the same reason, eat little and often, at least every four hours, to avoid sugar dips.

3 Get a massage. Muscle tension is a trigger, especially for people who are working hunched over a desk all day.

4 Research has shown that some migraine sufferers have a biochemical defect that affects their body's final handling of food containing amines. These include tyramine, which is found in cheese, wine and citrus fruits, and phenylethylamine, which is present in chocolate and alcohol. Amines are also absorbed more easily when fat is present, so skip fried food, chocolate and dairy.

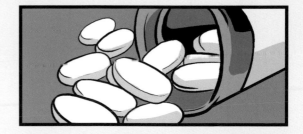

5 Pop some pills. At the first sign of symptoms, take aspirin or ibuprofen. Most find that these work better than paracetamol or codeine, especially if taken at an early stage.

6 Take triptans: these are not painkillers, but they can work well for migraines because they mimic serotonin.

HOW TO SURVIVE A
62 BACHELOR(ETTE) PARTY

Being sprayed blue and dressed up as a Smurf is fair enough, but to survive the entire night you're going to have to be careful about one thing: your self-respect.

1 Be the organiser. Sounds lame, but it will save you a lot of pain. Even if you're not the best man or maid of honour, step up with ideas. It means you can control the direction of the night.

2 Book ahead as much as you can. This is the only way you can guarantee your safety and sanity. Herding 15 drunks around in a city centre you don't know is hard enough; getting them into a club is a nightmare unless you book in advance.

3 Incorporate action into the day or night. People won't remember getting plastered in years to come, but they'll look back fondly on a moment when they faced their fears or went on a thrilling journey of discovery.

4 Be the one who takes the plunge first. If there is a challenge to be done, always be at the front of the queue. People will remember you long afterwards, and not as just a drinking buddy. If you fluff it, it's funnier to get it over with.

5 Build your day and night around food, not drink. Keep the focus on eating well and often to soften the impact of alcohol and keep people's behaviour under control. If it's your party, simply insist the others feed you.

6 Dressing up is fun, but it restricts your options. Book hotels near your venues so you can dash back to change at short notice. Take a photo of the hotel and street name before you leave, so you can always ask someone to help direct you back later on...

HOW TO SURVIVE A
PLANE CRASH

So many different things can, and do, go wrong on flights it's amazing that so few end up going pear-shaped. Other than praying and hoping for the best, here are some things you can do to help yourself should your plane take a nosedive.

1 Sit at the back. Rear seats are statistically safer in crashes, giving you a 40 per cent better chance of survival. First class isn't everything, you know.

2 Sit no more than five rows from an emergency exit, and always take note of how many rows away it is. If the plane is on fire, you have just 90 seconds' survival time. Choosing an aisle seat will mean you can exit faster.

3 Stay sober and awake for the first three minutes and the final eight minutes of your flight. Statistically, 80 per cent of crashes occur in these periods. Do not wear earphones or read at these moments.

4 There is rarely room to brace properly. Rest your head against your arms on the seat in front. Take sharp items out of your pockets. Place something soft under the chair in front to stop your legs breaking. Keep shoes laced tightly so they won't fall off.

5 Once the cabin crew has told you to, unbuckle and walk calmly to the exit without picking up baggage. If there is smoke impairing visibility, use the mental row count you took when you boarded to feel your way to the exit row.

6 If the emergency exit slides are activated, jump down one with your heels up and arms crossed over your chest. Ironically, many crash injuries occur when people get off the slide badly. Get out of the way at the bottom – they're designed to eject 70 people per minute.

HOW TO SURVIVE
64 YOUR COMMUTE

Let's face it, unless you have a limo or helicopter to ferry you around, commutes can be boring, stressful and unpleasant. The secret to alleviating the tedium is to make your journey work harder by incorporating small activities that actually leave your brain and body better off when you arrive.

1 Train surf. Stand without holding on to anything for as long as you can for a free workout. As you learn the bumps and bends on your route, you can bring your feet closer together until you eventually stand on one foot: pro level.

2 Boost your circulation and mood with some focused breathing: relax your shoulders and abdomen, then take a deep breath through your nose so your tummy expands. Hold, then exhale through a small hole in the mouth.

3 Use the 'five-more' rule to develop better concentration in your daily life. Force yourself to do five more things before you get distracted: remember five dates, sing five songs or plan your next five bucket-list holidays.

4 Network. Don't see other commuters as opponents: they could help your daily life. Make small talk, introduce yourself and share something like a newspaper or snack.

5 Start the working day early. Check emails and voicemail before you get in the car or train, and spend the journey mentally creating a checklist of tasks for the day. Write them down, or use your phone's voice memo app. This is the only time of the day when nobody from work can bother you.

6 Get off one stop early. Not only will the walk get your metabolism fired up, the mental exercise of navigating your way through new routes and avoiding obstacles will lead to higher productivity throughout the day.

HOW TO SURVIVE

65 SOMEONE WHO 'THINKS OUTSIDE THE BOX' IN MEETINGS

People want to outshine their peers in meetings, but sometimes style takes over from substance. Keep the jargon and waffle to a minimum by following a set of simple bluster-busting rules.

1 The braggart just wants to be heard, and to think they are the only one to come up with a breakthrough idea. Pander to their ego; recognise their brilliance at the start of the meeting and tell everyone else why their insights are going to be so crucial. That should shut them up.

2 It's up to you to build the rules: no jargon, no nonsense, no soliloquies. Just insights and actions. Make this clear from the start.

3 When someone starts talking nonsense, pick out one decent point they've raised, praise them for it, and direct a new question to another person immediately.

4 If they start again, remind everyone of the time and your next appointment. State clearly that you are moving on to the next item on the agenda, or simply keep referring to the original purpose of the meeting.

5 If you can't steer the meeting away from their verbal twaddle, distract them. Play with your phone. Raise your eyebrows comically, or act like a mosquito is circling you. Point at the clock on the wall, or show your watch to the person sitting next to you. Tapping the watch loudly is also good.

6 If they continue, just interrupt them. Start laughing uncontrollably at what they have just said, before fixing them with a stare and explicitly stating that their ideas are outdated and irrelevant. Next, swiftly ask the quietest person in the room what they think, congratulate them heartily for their insights, and wrap up the meeting.

HOW TO SURVIVE A
66 JELLYFISH STING

Jellyfish blooms are... well, blooming. Warmer global waters and fewer fishy predators means bumper numbers of the stinging saltwater creatures: when you get stung, make sure you know what to do.

1 Get out of the water immediately. Jellyfish rarely operate alone, and there will be more of the slippery suckers lurking in the water that you cannot see.

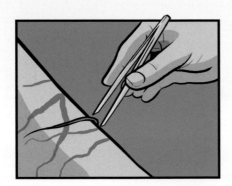

2 Remove any tentacles remaining on your skin using tweezers or a clean stick. Leaving them in place will make the sting worse.

3 If the pain is severe, call the emergency services immediately. Although rare, some stings, such as those of the box jellyfish, can be fatal. Better safe than sorry.

4 Don't urinate on the sting, or ask anyone else to sprinkle you with their special water. Despite its reputation, urine doesn't have the right chemical make-up to fix a jellyfish sting and it can actually make it feel worse by reacting badly with the cells that are injecting venom into your skin.

5 Instead, slowly pour sea water on the sting. Use cupped hands, or a child's bucket if you can. This will help to ease the pain (a bit). It's probably time to pack your bags and hail a cab.

6 When you get home, spread shaving cream over the skin on and around the sting. This will help prevent the spread of toxins. Apply an ice pack to reduce the pain and inflammation. Consider swapping boogieboarding for knitting...

HOW TO SURVIVE A
TRIP TO THE OPERA

For some, opera is just a fat lady, wearing a horned helmet, singing in a language they don't understand. But, if you know what you're watching, it can be a powerful experience.

1 Start with the ABC of opera: *Aïda*, *La bohème* or *Carmen*. These are the three most produced and lauded operas in the world, with iconic storylines and songs – if one of these doesn't get you hooked, nothing will.

2 Put the music on your sound system. In the same way a concert is more fun when you know the songs, an opera will be less intimidating if you recognise some of the tunes. Read the plot before the performance and it will be easier to sit back and enjoy the show.

3 Don't worry about brushing up on your Italian. Most opera houses these days have sur- or supertitles – translations that run above the stage or on the back of the seat in front of you. They sometimes also sing them in your language instead of the original, although some things can get lost in translation if you are used to the classic version.

4 Pick the right seat. Too close to the orchestra and the singing can be washed out by the music; too far away and it's hard to see the expressions on the singers' faces and really understand the emotion and nuance of their performances.

5 Bring binos. If all you can afford are the nose-bleed seats way up in the gods, bring a pair of binoculars. Tiny hi-tech ones are preferable to those gold antique specs on a stick you see in movies and many venues even sell or rent top-of-the line models.

6 Try opera with a twist. These days you can find everything from modern productions of Stephen King's *The Shining* or *The Manchurian Candidate* to an opera about JFK.

7 Dress up. While there is no strict dress code at most opera houses, you will stand out if you show up in a T-shirt or shorts. And for some, this is even that annual special occasion that calls for a tux or gown – so go to town and make a real night of it.

8 Pre-order your drinks and snacks so you don't have to join the scrum at the bar during the interval. Operas can be long, and you will probably get thirsty. Be aware, though, that it isn't good form to keep getting up to go to the loo, so avoid guzzling too much fluid.

9 If you find you really don't like the opera, don't just go home. Performances are often held in amazing buildings with great bars, so have a drink and make the most of the venue, even if you've had enough of the caterwauling.

HOW TO SURVIVE A
68 WILDFIRE

Wildfires are, well, wild – and not in a zany, fun way. Should you find yourself in the heat of the action, however, there are a few things you can do to help yourself.

1 Wildfires tend to create a wide, pear-shaped front that can move at up to 22.5kph (14mph). If it is dry, you're in a forest, you are uphill of the fire's advance and you're on foot, you're in shtuck. The blaze will be nearly impossible to outrun, and extremely dangerous to cross.

2 If you cannot see for smoke, do not attempt to run in the general direction of the wind. Hot air rising above the fire causes a powerful updraft, sucking air towards the front. These can even create vortices, small tornadoes that spread the fire in finger-like patterns.

3 Avoid any thick stands of trees or other vegetation. On hills, attempt to cross diagonally in front of the advancing flames, uphill and to one side, before descending the slope. This may bring you around to the side of the wildfire and let the leading edge of the blaze go past as it rages upwards.

4 Aim to reach a low, open point away from vegetation and lie down, breathing into your clothes to avoid inhaling hot gases. Once you're on flat land, run to find shelter.

5 A house will be safer than the open if the fire is spreading quickly, but only if there is no vegetation within 9m (30ft) of the property. In particular, pines, junipers, cedars and eucalyptus should be avoided– these trees generate many embers and are incendiary.

6 Trees further away from the house can in some cases serve as buffers against the fire, so check the width of the fire break when deciding whether to stay or go.

7 Inside the house, shut every window and remove curtains. Move all flammable furniture into the centre of the property. Close all internal doors. If possible set up a hose and/or sprinkler on the roof to douse the building for as long as you can. Switch off the gas supply.

69 HOW TO SURVIVE A
NUCLEAR EXPLOSION

So the worst has happened: a shock 10-kiloton nuclear detonation has just gone off. What do you do?

1 Shield your eyes. The initial flash will be enough to blind you from several miles away.

2 Fall face down on the floor, covering any exposed skin. Point your feet towards the detonation site. If you can, hide behind anything large and heavy, or in a grave-sized hole in the ground. Flash burns are likely if you are within 3km (2 miles) and in the line of sight of the bomb.

3 Wait several seconds for the pressure wave. This will flatten most objects within a few miles of ground zero, and send object flying past you before the wind sucks back in the opposite direction. Stay away from anything likely to fall over or be uprooted.

4 Still alive? You are now being bombarded with radiation and have a few hours at most before radioactive fallout starts raining from the sky. Get to shelter immediately, on foot. The detonation will affect electronics within 8km (5 miles), including car wiring.

5 If you can see the mushroom cloud, and make out the direction that the top is drifting in, run so that you are moving away from the 'tail' of fallout.

6 Head for high-quality shelter, such as an underground car park beneath a tower block or the sub-basement of a larger building. These offer 99.5 per cent protection. Windowless rooms centrally located on the middle floors of large buildings are also acceptable. The worst shelters are wood-frame bungalows.

7 Take off all your clothes and jewellery and throw them far away. Wash immediately with soap and shampoo. Do not use conditioner, which may lock radioactive particles to your hair. Do not scrub or break your skin. As a minimum, use wipes on skin that has been exposed outdoors. Find some uncontaminated clothes and wrap up completely. Blow your nose, wipe your eyelids, lashes and ears.

8 If you are in a low-quality shelter and there is a high-quality one within five minutes' run, head for it immediately. If a high-quality shelter is further away than that, you should set out no later than 30 minutes after detonation.

9 If you have no idea of where any better shelter might be found and you have no supplies, stay where you are for at least 24 hours. Then, if you are within 10–20 miles of ground zero, aim to get us far away as possible before you succumb to dehydration, hunger or your other injuries.

10 When you leave, head away from the blast zone using the fastest route possible. Avoid the direction of any military bases, centres of government, transport hubs, industrial or financial zones, refineries, power plants or chemical plants. Small rural towns and villages high up away from blast zones may offer the best combination of human assistance and remoteness. When you get there, destroy your clothing and wash again.

HOW TO SURVIVE
70 SMALL TALK

We've all been there – you're sitting at a table at a wedding with a load of strangers, or you're stuck in the elevator with only vaguely familiar colleagues. Stilted 'hello's and awkward nods over, you all lapse into a prolonged and agonising silence. What to do?

1 Look around you. If you are on or in anything that is moving (an escalator, an elevator, a queue for the toilets) keep the conversation short. If you don't, they'll get halfway through explaining their views on the upcoming election and you'll have to get off, get out or shut the cubical door in their face.

2 Use the free information you have to hand about the occasion or location you are both at as your opening gambit. If you're at a wedding, that's 'so how do you know the bride or groom?' If you're at a 5km-run, it's 'so is this the first one of these events you've done?' Open up questions that create points of connection.

3 Have (good) answers ready for broad questions. For example, 'how's work' should be answered with 'great, I'm looking forward to [insert appropriate anecdote in here]'. Do not give a closed answer. It's lazy.

4 Unless you know the answer to the question, don't ask it. 'How's your boyfriend?' might seem like a great opener, until you realise they ran off with the pool boy. 'Catch me up! What's new with work since I last saw you?' is less likely to lead you into a conversational cul-de-sac.

5 Lastly, you can master all of this and become a conversation ninja, but you cannot make people talk to you. If you get no response, cut your losses and run in the direction of the bar.

HOW TO SURVIVE A
FOOT-in-MOUTH SITUATION

Burying your head in the sand is the worst possible idea when you've dropped a clanger and said something you regret. Be prepared to take stock of the situation. Don't leave it too long or the situation will spiral out of control.

1 Assess how big the problem actually is. It often seems more significant to you than it appears to be from the outside. Talking it through with someone trusted allows you to regulate your response by taking on board an external perspective and modifying your actions accordingly.

2 Make a plan. Don't just react to events. What you do next could affect your life and reputation forever. Don't think about what will happen in the next hour. Think about the next year. How do you want to look back on this situation and remember it? How do you want others to recall it in a year's time? Act on that long-term basis.

3 The way you respond must be in keeping with what people expect of you. If you act out of character, it shows you're either likely to make more errors, or that you've been living a lie and this is the real you.

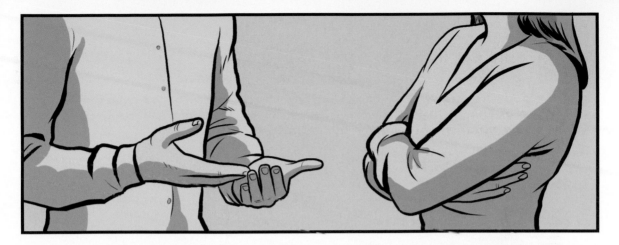

4 If you've made a mistake, admit it. Things will go on longer if you don't. Saying sorry, explaining what you're going to do to put it right and, even better, actually showing you've started to do something already, is the best way to do it. Tension is removed by apologising, sincerely.

5 In crisis-management practice, responding in a professional way can actually enhance your reputation by demonstrating you know your faults and can work to fix them. The same can apply to your personal life, too.

HOW TO SURVIVE
72 TIME TRAVEL

Time travel doesn't exist solely in the realms of fantasy – going forwards in time is perfectly possible according to existing laws of physics. Surviving the journey is, however, another matter...

1 Time slows for any moving object: someone who has made weekly transatlantic flights for 40 years has shifted $\frac{1}{1000}$ of a second into the future. If you want to progress any further, however, you are going to need to travel very, very fast. If you were to move at 30,000kps (18,628mps) for 10 years you'd end up just three weeks further on.

2 The alternative method of beating the clock is to warp space–time itself using a wormhole: a singularity in which gravity has distorted the fabric of reality, allowing you to move forwards and backwards in time and space. Forwards, no problem. But back in time? You need to cope with a few paradoxes.

3 So, you find yourself back in ye goode olde days. Don't do anything that would contradict the reality of the moment in time from which you have come (the 'present reality'). Like shooting your grandfather. This is known as an 'inconsistent causal loop'.

4 Instead, try out a 'consistent causal loop', like putting money in a compound interest account while you are in the past. This changes the present reality, but does not destroy it.

5 Prepare for weird things to happen. The 'post-selected model' says that you can't create a past event that contradicts your present: something will always stop you.

6 There is a chance that you might travel into a 'parallel universe', which involves moving along a separate timeline to your present reality. Here you will be able to create inconsistencies and contradictions – but you probably won't ever find your way back again.

HOW TO SURVIVE

73 PREPARING LOBSTER (AND EATING IT IN STYLE)

So, you have a hot date coming over and you want to impress by cooking up a crustacean and dismembering it with panache. Here's how to do it...

1 Purchase one live lobster and a sense of humour. Allow 800g–1kg (1lb 12oz–2lb 2oz) per person. Look for an active dude (read: the one making a break for freedom) with bright eyes and no marks on its body.

2 Pop the lobster in the freezer for a couple of hours to knock it out, well, cold, then swiftly dispatch it by sticking the point of a sharp knife through the cross on its head. Cook the critter for 15 minutes in a pan of boiling water with 1 tbs sea salt per 1L (1.7 pints) of water.

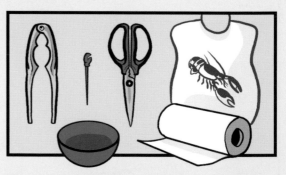

3 Assemble your tools. A seafood (or nut) cracker, a toothpick, kitchen scissors, a bib, a bowl for shells and enough paper towels to stock a nursery. Oh, and that sense of humour.

4 There are three main sections: the claws, body and tail (where most of the meat is to be found). Work head to tail for optimum efficiency. Remove the claws by twisting them away from the body. Crack 'em and pick 'em. This is the most fiddly bit done. Have a stiff drink.

5 Remove the tail with a delicate twist of the wrist. Watch out for after-spray, there's a lot of juice. Turn the tail over and, using scissors, cut along either side of the under-shell. Lift back and take out the meat. Chuck out the black digestive tract.

6 Finally, twist off the legs and loosen the meat with a toothpick. Suck it out; this is dead sexy (not) and will make you look like a pro.

Learn how to speak the language of dogs, and know when to stay out of their way. Size and breed play no part in how friendly or otherwise a mutt is. Aggressive behaviour is almost always the result of too little exposure to different people on a regular basis.

1 Do not disturb a dog that's on the job. Dogs often attack when they're looking after what they consider a 'high-value resource', such as a yard, puppies or even a bone.

2 Let sleeping dogs lie. Old sayings stick around for a reason – dogs that are sleeping are very easily startled.

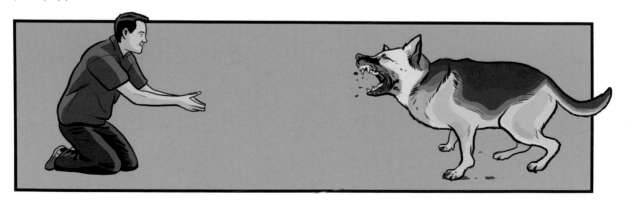

3 Spot a bad dog from a block away. A dog that's pointed directly at you, very still, with a hunched back and ears pricked up, should be avoided.

4 Be wary of a wagging tail. If it's a slow and steady wag, level with the dog's back, it's probably happy to see you. But a tail that's wagging low and fast is a sign of nervousness; a high wag is a sign of arousal – both can be signs of aggression.

5 Go in slow and low. Turn slightly to the side, reach your hand out below its face, giving it a few seconds to smell you, then pet its neck or chest. Never go in over the top of its head.

6 If it bites, back away. The first nip is usually a warning, which will give you a chance to get to safety. The fearsome latch-and-shake is very rare, but if it does happen, fight like hell. If you're losing, curl up in a ball facing the ground to protect your stomach, organs and face, with both fists over the back of your neck.

75 HOW TO SURVIVE A CROWD STAMPEDE

The main danger in a stampede comes from 'compressive asphyxia', whereby pressure on the lungs and abdomen prevents you from breathing. This is exactly the means used by a boa constrictor to kill its prey: it's pretty lethal!

1 If people are just moving in a dense crowd, you shouldn't panic unless pushing begins. Five people leaning against one can achieve a pressure of 5420 Newtons – enough to break ribs and collapse lungs.

2 If you can't avoid travelling through the crowd – say, you're exiting a burning building – then stay central to the crowd's mass. Do not try to go around the side to get further ahead. It is more dangerous to be stuck between the crowd and a wall.

3 If there is a pillar or another obstacle ahead, try to move towards it. It will cause a natural 'bubble' in the pressure of the crowd – like shaking a ketchup bottle – and it will be safer on the other side. Ellipsoid shapes are better for this than square or round obstacles.

4 The crowd will be moving towards a focal point: a bridge, or emergency exit, perhaps. The closer you are to this, the more intense the forward motion becomes. If you feel your feet being raised off the ground during the motion of the crowd, then get ready to abandon your position.

5 The crowd will naturally push forwards and then ebb backwards. Wait for the next backwash of movement and, when it comes, step back and to one side, like a crab. The pressure in the crowd releases radially, so moving diagonally outwards rather than backwards will ease the blockage faster.

76

HOW TO SURVIVE
A FREE-FALLING ELEVATOR

So, the elevator is plummeting. You only have a few seconds before impact. Luckily, air pressure below the lift may stop it from reaching truly devastating speeds. The impact may still be comparable to being hit by a moving car, though: you need protection.

1 Do not attempt to jump just before landing in order to lessen the impact. The reduction will be so small as to be insignificant, and you may even hit your head on the ceiling of the elevator, before crumpling back down.

2 Do not prostrate yourself on the floor to spread out your weight. On impact, lying down flat means that your brain will be travelling at the same speed as the lift. You have to increase the distance over which your brain can decelerate.

3 If the elevator is small or crowded, brace yourself for impact by standing with slightly bent knees. This turns your legs into a 'crumple zone' that will absorb most of the impact, protecting your vital organs.

4 If you have bags with you, stand on them. Stack up suitcases and use them as a podium. This will give you even more space in which to decelerate when the lift lands. Wrap your head and face in your coat or jumper if you have time, to protect them from falling debris.

5 If there are handrails, use them to brace yourself. Spread your weight as much as possible to slow your impact. You may break or at least dislocate your arms, and your legs are almost certainly going to fracture, but, looking on the bright side, by doing this you will stand a better chance of protecting your brain and living to tell the tale.

77

HOW TO SURVIVE A
JOB YOU HATE

When the going gets tough, the tough hide under the table... or not; you can't hide under your desk forever. If you really loathe your job, you have two choices: resign, or make your job better. However, even if you choose to leave, it's always worth trying to negotiate first.

1 Timing is crucial. The best moment to speak to your boss is after lunch, with a coffee, and with them seated in a comfortable chair. All three of these factors will maximise your psychological influence over them.

2 Don't beat around the bush. Ask straight out for more than you need. The more you ask for, the more you end up getting. Substantial demands influence the agenda from the start, up their expectations and give you more wriggle room.

3 Watch your boss's body language for signs of discomfort. If they touch their neck, withdraw their chin, bite their lips or even wring their hands, they are reaching their limit; do not press harder. Be confident, not pushy.

4 Use silence as your weapon. Allow them the time to stew over what you have said. Explain your terms, state your offer and then wait for them to respond.

5 Don't take no for an answer. Ask for the reasons for the negative response and knock down each one in turn. Turn a flat refusal into several smaller obstacles: obstacles can generally be surmounted...

6 Know when to quit. If they make an offer that's less than what you need to stay, walk away. Successful negotiations are always about achieving a win/win situation for everyone, and if you are always going to be the loser then it's time to fetch your coat.

HOW TO SURVIVE
78 AS A WOMAN IN A MALE-DOMINATED INDUSTRY (AND VICE VERSA)

For all we'd like the world to be a fair place, in some jobs not all genders are created equal and you have to fight like hell if you happen to be the minority. Here's how.

1 Be good at your job. Personality clashes arise irrespective of the gender of you and your boss. Your boss may just not like you very much, or be a total pig to everyone. Doing your job well in a way only you can is the best way to rise above this.

2 Relish being the outsider. You're in a unique position and don't need to try that hard to cultivate a distinctive identity, so turn yourself into the go-to person for things only you can know about.

3 Be aware of your office's views on commitment and productivity. Some value presenteeism (putting in the hours, and making sure your boss and colleagues see you doing so). Others prefer social players (those who get stuck into extra-curricular activities).

4 Don't be a pretender. Just because you roar along with the office banter, go to the socials and ingratiate yourself as one of the 'lads'/'girls', you're not fooling *anyone*. People who behave counter-stereotypically can experience a backlash. Authenticity is key.

5 Find a mentor at work. Somebody who will teach you how to manage difficult situations and who will bring new opportunities your way. They don't have to be of the same sex as you, but it might help.

6 Get loud. Once your position in the team is cemented, shout. Not in a petulant or autocratic way – but make sure your ideas are heard. Be vocal in meetings or book time with your boss to debate concerns and offer solutions. You'll be in the power seat before you know it.

79 HOW TO SURVIVE IN A DYSFUNCTIONAL FAMILY

Psychoanalytic theory says every family is a system, within which members unconsciously fulfil a role (think Homer as buffoon, Marge as home-builder, Bart as wild child, Lisa as goody two-shoes swot and Maggie as the forgotten one). Dysfunction happens when people's roles affect the purpose and running of the system.

1 Identify your unconscious role within the family. Are you the breadwinner, black sheep, the perfect one or the screw-up? If you find it unhelpful being labelled in this way, resist the stereotype by acting out of role.

2 Identify the unconscious role others may be playing in your family; challenge this by enabling them to act differently and getting others in the family to stop characterising them in this way.

3 Sit down together and identify the primary task of your family 'system'. Take stock: see how you're getting on and where you could improve.

4 If you're an adult, you can distance yourself from your childhood family group and start your own, both geographically and emotionally. Try to pinpoint what went wrong with your parents and siblings as it will help you to avoid repeating the same dynamics again with your spouse and kids.

5 Seek help: family therapy, video interaction guidance between two family members, or solo counselling can all help. Just one person changing can alter the family dynamics.

6 Take heart from the concept of being a 'good-enough' family and try not to live up to some media representation of 'perfection'. There is no such thing.

HOW TO SURVIVE
80 THE FIRST DAY OF THE SALES

Consumerism gone bad or the sign of a thriving market economy, the one thing you can be sure about is that seasonal sales are crazy. But you don't need to be. Instead of camping outside the stores and waiting to get beaten up like the rest of the bargain-crazed world, you can get smart.

1 Start early. Many January sales now start online on Christmas Eve, and many Black Friday 'offers' have turned out to be nothing of the kind – so keep scanning the internet.

2 It's only a bargain if you need it. Ask yourself truthfully if you're going to use it. If you can afford it, make a list of the things you actually need and try to stick to it.

3 Think about the previous year's weather. Long summers mean stockists will slash prices on coats, boots and jumpers. Bad summers mean you'll get the best prices on garden and outdoor leisure gear.

4 Keep your head. Although many retailers will discount by as much as 70 per cent, always compare prices first using online shopping comparison tools before you buy.

5 Buy online. Stores may be offering a few loss-leading items to tempt you in, but the discounts are unlikely to be worth the hassle of waiting in the cold for hours and then trying to wrestle the item off a shrieking grandma. How long would it take you to earn that discount at work? And how much would you pay someone to take your place at the store?

6 Make big purchases on a credit card you pay off in full every month. That way, when you realise you've made a silly mistake buying those flimsy discounted designer dog sunglasses, you stand a better chance of getting a refund.

HOW TO SURVIVE
81 IN A MINEFIELD

It's quite hard to tell that you're in a minefield until it's too late – they are either generally nearly impossible to access, or they aren't signposted at all... If you do find yourself in one and have yet to be blown to smithereens, however, then a methodical approach is essential if you want to make it out in one piece.

1 Lie down on your stomach. Keep your elbows in as much as possible and begin to drag your body very slowly forwards. This spreads your weight, protects you from the blast of nearby mines going off, and gives you the best view of booby traps ahead.

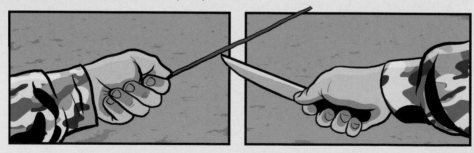

2 Use a tripwire detector (should you happen to have one!) with your left hand. This is a long, thin, lightweight piece of wire with which you can gently check the air ahead of you. *Very* gently, please.

3 With your right hand, use a long spike – a large knife will do – to probe the soil in an arc in front of you. Be methodical, prodding at a shallow angle every 5cm (2in). Clear a path at least 0.5m (1½ft) wide to pass through.

4 If you feel anything, gently place a flag, stick or cane in the ground to mark it. Go around the obstacle, inching forwards and using the tripwire detector and spike. Slowly.

5 Don't try to defuse anything. Your aim is to get out of the minefield as safely and quickly as you can. The build-up of stress will cloud your judgement, so focus solely on probing, flagging up dangers and inching onwards.

6 When you exit the minefield, help others evacuate using your route and leave a mark or sign to warn people. Contact the local police immediately.

HOW TO SURVIVE
BUMPING INTO YOUR EX

Want to stay friends but don't know how? Take the pressure off the next time you find yourself tongue-tied in front of your previous partner.

1 Talk about new things you're doing to show them you have expanded as a person (hopefully not literally). Don't ask about any current relationships: it implies that you might still be interested.

2 Don't dwell on your new partner's greatness. Tell your ex things are going fine and move on to the next topic. If you are single, let them know you are enjoying it but don't go into detail about just how much fun you are having.

3 If you're happy with the way things are going, suggest going for coffee, not a vat of wine. Or suggest doing something with friends but make sure your chums are aware, from the start, that this is not a matchmaking exercise.

4 During the encounter, scroll through a mental tick list of all the annoying things they did. It will make you smile, feel relieved and break your nerves. If you are feeling fragile, write down their faults and look at them when you are on a bathroom break.

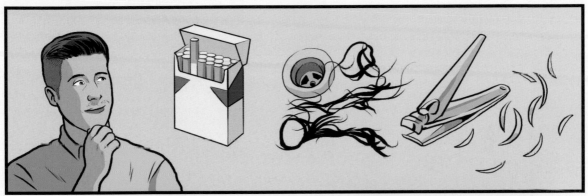

5 Wear the clothes that you know you look good in, but they never liked. It reminds you that you are free to do what you want — and lets them know you don't value their opinion as much anymore.

6 If they start bringing up the past, or even getting flirty, steer the conversation in another direction. Everyone likes to play the coquette, but if you indulge in it you might get carried away and give the wrong impression. And you could even end up back in their bed — which isn't what you want.

HOW TO SURVIVE
83 GETTING KIDNAPPED

When it comes to kidnapping, the motives of the bad guys are the key to whether or not you will make it. If you have been taken for political terrorism reasons, the bad news is that dialogue, and your survival, is unlikely. If, however, you have merely been snatched to be held for ransom, as a human shield or because someone has gone crazy, then negotiations are more plausible and you may just make it. Phew.

1 If you're in a group kidnap situation and 30 minutes have passed without any killings, negotiators act on the assumption that the hostage-takers will not murder anyone. If they do slaughter someone, then it's likely a tactical team will launch an assault very soon. Take cover if you can.

2 Help calm things down and let your captors contain the situation. If you're able to talk to them safely, let them get their point across repeatedly. Suspend judgement, focus the attention on them and allow them to achieve a more rational frame of mind.

3 Try to keep kidnappers problem-solving for as long as possible. Once verbalised, their demands can suddenly seem disproportionate, even absurd, and a negotiated exit strategy – the 'ladder down' – is more achievable.

4 Drive the conversation in unrelated directions to distract them. Keep asking what they want, how they want it, why they thought of it, to whom they are going to issue demands, etc.

5 Some negotiators advise speaking to just one of the kidnappers, to isolate them. When, inevitably, the demands are not met, the other kidnappers may turn on the segregated person, deflecting their anger from you. Most hostage situations are over in less than a day: let the takers play themselves out.

HOW TO SURVIVE
84 BEING STRUCK BY LIGHTNING

The odds of being struck by lightning are about one in a million. If you happen to be that special person, the good news is you have a 90 per cent chance of survival – as long as the strike is indirect.

1 Avoid a *direct* strike at all costs: the chances of surviving that are a slim million to one. The average bolt carries 500MJ of energy – enough to boil 250 gallons of water instantly – and can strike from as far away as 16km (10 miles).

2 Urban environments are the safest place to be during a lightning storm. Buildings and cars channel a bolt's energy around you and to the ground, an effect called the Faraday Cage. Stay away from obvious electricity conductors such as telephones, which account for most of the shocks received indoors during storms.

3 When a storm is forecast, avoid open spaces such as beaches, golf courses and lakes. You will often be the tallest point in these environments and there may be little shelter. Fishing poles, golf clubs, umbrellas or anything else that may act as lightning 'bait' should be jettisoned immediately.

4 If you must stand in the open for hours waving around a metal stick, check weather reports in advance or at least seek shelter at the very first signs of storm clouds.

5 Get to know the 'flash-bang' rule. Every five seconds between the flash of lightning and the crack of thunder equates to 1.6km (1 mile) between you and the lightning. The shorter the time between them, the closer the storm is getting.

6 If lightning is less than 1.6km (1 mile) away, immediately assume the lightning position: crouch with your feet close together to close the 'arc', at least 9m (30ft) from anyone else. Place anything that can provide insulation – a sleeping pad, picnic mat, backpack – between you and the ground. Remain in this position until the lightning, once again, is at least 1.6km (1 mile) away.

7 Nowhere is more dangerous than the high-mountain backcountry, which is the site of most lightning deaths. In this environment, never travel up high in the afternoon (when most lightning storms roll through) and, if you are caught out, immediately descend, seek out a dip or ravine in flat terrain, and get away from lone trees.

8 While a lone tree is to be avoided, a large stand of evenly tall trees can provide shelter, as the bolt will not be able to distinguish a single high point. If someone is hit by a bolt from the blue, first check for breathing and a pulse and begin CPR, if necessary. Don't worry, victims do not retain a charge. Lightning strikes are like a fibrillator turned up to 11 and can short out our respiratory and nervous systems.

HOW TO SURVIVE A
85 DIGITAL DETOX

Scientists say that digital multitasking is actually making us dumber. So ditch the devices, re-learn how to do one thing at a time, and do it well.

1 Admit you have a problem. A dependence on technology and e-connectedness is officially a diagnosable addiction, and recognising that you may be overdoing it is step one. Not sure? Download an app (natch) that tracks your non-work screen time – more than four hours a day has been shown to cause anxiety and depression.

2 Begin your detox by designating a set amount of time – no less than a day, several, if possible – and notify everyone who needs to know that you will be officially off the radar and not contactable during this period. Weekends or vacations are particularly good choices.

3 Make plans for your time off from tech. Boredom is one of the biggest triggers for picking up that smartphone or tablet. Fill your day with hands-on activities or social situations in which you won't be tempted to turn to your tech. Nature is a particularly good antidote and offers powerful perspective, so take a hike. (Actually, if you do take a hike, it may be an idea to take a phone...)

4 Get through the first few hours. The period immediately after switching off is the toughest. But those feelings of anxiety will subside, especially if you jump right into other activities and keep yourself busy.

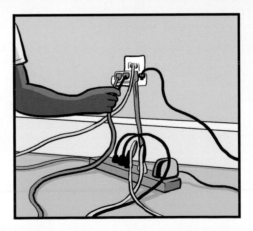

5 Plug back in slowly. Ease back into your digital life with clear pre-set boundaries about how often you will check voicemails, emails and social-media sites, and when it's appropriate. If old habits start to creep back in, nip it in the bud with another detox.

THE ODDS OF DYING FROM...

Risk? It's all relative.

Here's what you should really be worrying about. The bigger the circle, the higher the chances of kicking the bucket...

The odds of getting a hole in one are 1 in 5,000.

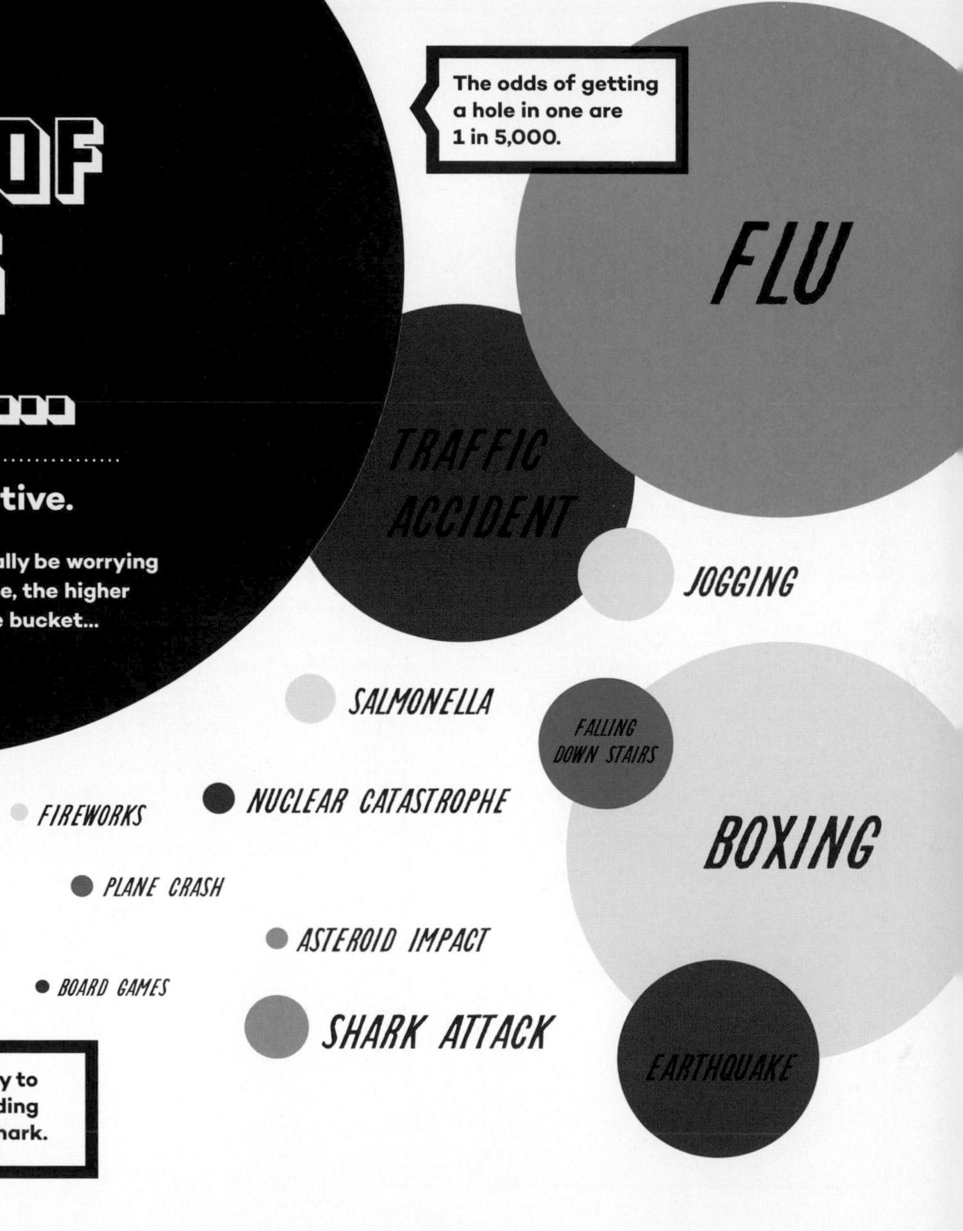

FLU

TRAFFIC ACCIDENT

JOGGING

SALMONELLA

FALLING DOWN STAIRS

BOXING

FIREWORKS

NUCLEAR CATASTROPHE

SMALLPOX
Zero chance.
(Officially eradicated in 1980)

PLANE CRASH

ASTEROID IMPACT

BOARD GAMES

SHARK ATTACK

EARTHQUAKE

You are more likely to be killed by a vending machine than a shark.

You have a 1 in 25,000 chance of getting stuck in an elevator.

HEART DISEASE

The single biggest killer worldwide.
(Responsible for one in every five deaths)

LIGHTNING STRIKE

GUNSHOT WOUND

You are more likely to be killed by a donkey than in a plane crash.

CANCER

DOG ATTACK

CLIMBING
(above 6000m)

You have a 1 in 36 chance of rolling a pair of sixes.

One in 10 premature deaths is caused by inactivity.

THE ILLUSTRATOR

Rob Dobi is an illustrator from Trumbull, CT. He lives with his wife Christina, his dog Buddy and a lifelong struggle with poor eating habits. He has future plans of publishing a book on how to survive illustrating a book about how to survive various scenarios. More of his work can be viewed at http://robdobi.com.

THE AUTHORS

Robin Barton is an award-winning author, editor and journalist who contributes to national media in the UK, the US and Australia. He enjoys beer, bikes and books.

Ed Chipperfield is a writer and journalist. A regular contributor to *The Sunday Times* and *Men's Health*, Ed has survived riding bulls, climbing volcanoes, taking a bath with 25 live rattlesnakes and building his own house. He now lives in it, minus the rattlesnakes.

Will Cockrell is a writer and editor living in Brooklyn, NY. He spent ten years working as an outdoor guide; his most recent staff position was as Articles Editor at Men's Journal magazine in the U.S.

Amy Grier is currently features editor at *Women's Health* magazine, and has previously worked at *Stylist* and *ES Magazine*. She enjoys cooking, eating, shouting at the TV and, if all else fails, can usually be found buried in knitwear watching a David Attenborough documentary on catch-up TV.

Jonathan Thompson is a former Senior Editor of *Men's Health* magazine, now a freelance journalist contributing style and travel features to titles including the *Daily Telegraph*, the *Guardian*, *Tatler*, *Esquire* and *Conde Nast Traveller*. He recently visited all 50 States of America in a month, and has the dubious accolade of being the UK's most experienced male wingwalker.

ACKNOWLEDGEMENTS

With thanks to our survival experts....

33 Engineer Regiment Army Bomb Disposal Unit
(pp 204–205)

American Association of Dermatologists (pp 106–107)

Larry Amsel, Assistant Professor of Clinical Psychology,
Columbia University, College of physicians and surgeons
(pp 54–57)

Marc Ashdown, presenter, BBC London TV News
(pp 136–137)

F. Diane Barth, Psychotherapist, *Psychology Today* blog
(pp 94–95)

Simon Barwell, wedding planner, www.tyingtheknot.org
(pp 160–161)

Elliot Bennett, Autoimmunology Biomedical Scientist
(pp 104–105)

Lucy Beresford, psychotherapist and author of *Happy
Relationships at Home, Work & Play* (McGraw-Hill
Professional, 2013) www.lucyberesford.co.uk
(pp 60–61 and 196–197)

Todd Bosse, Disaster Management Specialist, Pacific
Disaster Center, HI (pp 32–35)

Lynn Brennan, owner of Business Etiquette International
(pp 112–113)

Caroline Brealey, founder of Mutual Attraction,
www.mutualattraction.co.uk (pp 30–31)

British Association of Dermatologists (pp 106–107)

Cathy Brown, Former European Boxing Champion,
Personal Trainer at The Third Space Gym in London,
www.cathybrown.co.uk; www.thethirdspace.com (pp 118–119)

Dan Buettner, author of *The Blue Zones*
(National Geographic Society, 2012) (pp 156–157)

Karl Bushby, Brit currently walking around the world
(pp 46–47)

John Clayton, clinical and medical hypnotherapist,
psychotherapist and NLP trainer, The Pinnacle Practice,
Nottingham and London, Harley Street (pp 48–51)

Brian Clegg, author of *How to Build a Time Machine*
(Griffin, 2013) (pp 186–187)

Professor Angela Clow, University of Westminster
(pp 156–157)

Philip Coulter, Head Chef, Wright Brothers Oyster and Porter
House, www.thewrightbrothers.co.uk (pp 188–189)

Professor George Crooks, NHS 24 Medical Director
(pp 168–169)

Louise Daniel, Matron at Spire The Glen Hospital, Bristol
(pp48–51)

Chris Davis, Medical Director, Altitude and Mountain
Medicine Consultants, a branch of the Travel, Expedition
and Altitude Medicine (TEAM) Clinic, University of Colorado
School of Medicine (p122–123)

Ann Demarais, First Impressions Consulting, New York
(pp 74–77)

Eric Down, Senior Style Editor at *Men's Health* magazine
(pp78–79)

Debra Fine, author of *The Fine Art of Small Talk*
(Piatkus, 2014) (pp 30–31 and 182–183)

The research team at Football Manager 2015
(www.footballmanager.com) (pp 150–151)

Professor Robert Friedman, Department of Dermatology,
New York University (pp 40–41)

Peter Grove, founder of National Curry Week (@supportcurry) and author of *The Flavours of History* (Godiva Books, 2011) (pp 124–125)

Steve Harrison, personal trainer (pp 164–165)

Lizzy Hawker, British ultramarathon runner and founder of the Ultra Tour Monte Rosa (www.ultratourmonterosa.com) (pp 138–141)

Jonathan Hemus, director of Insignia reputation and crisis management consultancy (www.insigniacomms.com) (pp 184–185)

Stuart Holt, Metropolitan Opera of New York City (pp 170–173)

Ryan Horner, LTR Training Systems, www.survivaltraining.com (pp 18–21)

Journal of Sports Sciences (www.tandfonline.com) (pp 150–151)

Rob Kendall, author of *Blamestorming: Why Conversations Go Wrong and How to Fix Them* (Watkins Publishing, 2014) (pp 30–31 and 180–181)

Dan Keyler, snake envenomation expert(pp 58–59)

Keith Knudsen, Deputy Director of the Earthquake Science Center, USGS (pp 12–13)

Wempy Dyota Koto, CEO of business-development agency Wardour and Oxford (www.wardourandoxford.com) (pp 166–167)

Charlie Lambros, Fashion Editor at *Women's Health* magazine (pp 78–79)

Kimberley Lauf, British Airways spokeswoman and customer service manager (c/o BA press office) (pp 38–39)

Rachel MacLynn, psychologist and founder of Vida Consultancy introduction agency, www.thevidaconsultancy.com (pp 30–31)

Dr Emma Mardlin, Clinical and Medical hypnotherapist, psychotherapist and NLP trainer, The Pinnacle Practice, Nottingham and London, Harley Street (pp 48–51)

Rick Mastracchio, NASA astronaut, 1996–present, 9 spacewalks (pp 14–17)

Amelia McCloskey, vocal coach (pp 152–153)

Major Owen McGrane, U.S. Army, Emergency Medicine Physician (pp 100–101)

Nick Midworth, commercial director at advertising agency OgilvyAction (pp 196–197)

Migraine Action (pp 158–159)

The Migraine Trust (pp 158–159)

Michael Moran, Chief Executive of Fairplace (pp 156–157)

Joe Mulligan, British Red Cross Head of First Aid (pp 168–169)

National Migraine Centre (pp 158–159)

New England Journal of Medicine (pp 156–157)

Todd Offenbacher, Director of the Sierra Avalanche Center, CA (pp 108–111)

David Palmerton, FAA plane-crash expert (pp 162–163)

Popular Mechanics (pp 162–163)

Steve Quarles, Center for Fire Research and Outreach at Berkeley's Richmond Field Station (pp 174–177)

Dr Nerina Ramlakhan, psychologist (pp 164–165)

Kirsten Rechnitz, advanced instructor, Boulder Outdoor Survival School, UT (pp52–53 and 130–131)

Susan RoAne, author of *How To Work a Room* (WmMorrowPB, 2007) (pp 112–113)

Proceedings of the Royal Society, http://rspa.royalsocietypublishing.org/content/470/2163/20130693 (pp 178–181)

Sarah Ryan, head of matchmaking at Elect Club dating service (www.electclub.co.uk) (pp 206–207)

Neil Sadick, clinical professor of dermatology, Cornell national board of hair loss www.sadickdermatology.com (pp 44–45)

Harvey Schlossberg, NYPD hostage negotiator (pp 208–209)

Deborah Shanahan, Senior Deals Researcher at MoneySavingExpert (pp 202–203)

Michael Sincere, author of *Understanding Stocks* (McGraw-Hill, 2014); *Predict the Next Bull or Bear Market and Win* (Adams Media, 2014); and *Understanding Options* (McGraw-Hill, 2006) (pp 128–129)

SK:N clinic (pp 106–107)

Noel 'Razor' Smith, associate editor of *Inside Time* (pp 154 155)

Victor Sojo, post-doctoral research fellow, Centre for Ethical Leadership, Ormond College, The University of Melbourne (pp 198–199)

Stanford Encyclopedia of Philosophy (pp 186–187)

Professor Keith Still, Crowd Dynamics Ltd (pp 192–193)

Adam Swisher, NOLS instructor (pp 210–213)

Dr Bob Taibbi, licensed clinical social worker and author (pp 64–65)

Ros Taylor, business psychologist and author of *Creativity at Work*, www.rostaylorcompany.com (pp 126–127)

Dave Thomas, ex-SAS negotiator and MD of Spy Games training (pp 196–197)

Alex Thomson, Britain's most successful solo round-the-world sailor, www.alexthomsonracing.com (pp 142–143)

Adele Tobias, child psychologist (pp 68–71 and 198–199)

Steve Toporoff, Attorney, Federal Trade Commission, USA, Individual Privacy and Identity Protection (pp 72–73)

Dr Paul Torrens, Arizona State University (pp192–193)

The University of Bath (www.bath.ac.uk) (pp 150–151)

University of Illinois Physics Department, LiveScience (pp194–195)

Jo Usmar, co-author of *This Book Will Make You Mindful* (Quercus, 2015) (pp 114–117)

Kristopher VanOver, Animal Behaviour and Training Specialist, ASPCAL.A., CPBT (Certified Professional Dog Trainer (KA: Knowledge Assessed)) (pp 190 191)

Dr Andrew Westwood, Asst Prof. Clinical Neurology, Columbia University (pp 98–99)

Jonathan Wilde, *GQ* magazine (US) (pp82–83)

Tiffany Wright, Director & Romance Planner, www.theoneromance.com (pp 206–207)

Genevieve Zawada, CEO of Elect Club dating service (www.electclub.co.uk) (pp 206–207)

Other sources:

'Energy metabolism of ALS patients', www.ncbi.nlm.nih.gov/pubmed/1909943 (pp 104–105)

'Planning Guidance for Response to a Nuclear Detonation'; US Department of Homeland Security guidance (pp 178–181)

www.irunfar.com/2012/09/your-ultra-training-bag-of-tricks-the-difficult-art-of-peaking (pp 138–141)

www.ready.gov/nuclear-blast (pp 178–181)

INDEX

Published in April 2015 by Lonely Planet Publications Pty Ltd
ABN 36 005 607 983
www.lonelyplanet.com
ISBN 978 1 74360 752 7
© Lonely Planet 2015
Printed in China

Foreword © Ed Stafford
Photos © Keith Ducatel (p7 top), Getty Images (p8),
Pete McBride (p6, p7 bottom)

Publishing Director Piers Pickard
Commissioning Editor Jessica Cole
Art Direction Claire Clewley
Illustrator Rob Dobi
Layout Designer Louise Leffler
Editor Lucy Doncaster
Pre-press production Tag Publishing
Print production Larissa Frost

Thanks to Ryan Evans, Jen Feroze

Lonely Planet offices
AUSTRALIA
90 Maribyrnong St, Footscray, Victoria, 3011, Australia
Phone 03 8379 8000 Email talk2us@lonelyplanet.com.au
USA
150 Linden St, Oakland, CA 94607
Phone 510 250 6400 Email info@lonelyplanet.com
UNITED KINGDOM
240 Blackfriars Road London SE1 8NW
Phone 020 8433 1333 Email go@lonelyplanet.co.uk

FSC MIX
Paper from responsible sources
FSC™ C021741
www.fsc.org

Paper in this book is certified against the Forest Stewardship
Council™ standards. FSC™ promotes environmentally
responsible, socially beneficial and economically viable
management of the world's forests.